February 13, 1984

To Ellary:

Hope you find my exploits as a management consultant interesting reading.

Wishing you the very best,

Sincerely,

Jerome N. Fuchs

MANAGEMENT
CONSULTANTS
IN ACTION

MANAGEMENT CONSULTANTS IN ACTION

JEROME H. FUCHS

HAWTHORN BOOKS, INC.
Publishers/New York

I keep six honest serving-men
(They taught me all I knew);
Their names are What and Why and When
And How and Where and Who.

Rudyard Kipling
The Elephant's Child

Contents

	Introduction	1
1	Two Hats and a Hundred Hands	9
2	Made of Iron	20
3	From Little Acorns Grow Mighty Oaks—Sometimes!	35
4	Batten Down the Hatches	57
5	A Thousand and One Nights of Good Salesmanship	68
6	The Anatomy of a Turnaround	89
7	Profit Improvement Pays Off	110
8	Valhalla, Shangri-La, Utopia, and The Land of Oz	128
9	Red Dog	150
10	Topsy Never Made it Big	164
11	If You've Seen One, You've Seen Them All	181
12	The Management Consultant's Smorgasbord	194
	Index	211

Introduction

Management Consultants in Action is the inside story of management consulting—one of the least known and fastest growing businesses in the United States. In three decades this profession has expanded so rapidly that, at the present time, there is one consultant for every hundred salaried managers in business. And from all indications, this ratio will get smaller as we move farther into the supersonic seventies.

In prehistoric times (B.C.—Before Consultants), men such as Sir Richard Arkwright, Matthew Robinson Boulton, James Watt, Jr., and Charles Babbage invented ingenious labor-saving devices. These early creative whizzes influenced this branch of the industrial revolution from the mid-1700s through the end of the nineteenth century. Then, in the age of "renaissance" from 1890 to 1915, the efficiency expert was born. Frederick Taylor, the father of scientific management, started it all when he applied common sense and a systematic approach to problem solving.

One of Taylor's most notable achievements took place at the Midvale Steel Company, where a ragtag crew was employed to shovel coal into the open hearth furnaces. The men used shovels of various sizes; and as a result of the differences in their tools, some of them were able to work more efficiently than others. Through an intensive study, Taylor determined that a standard shovel thirty-six inches long, weighing eight pounds, and having a square shape, could lift forty pounds of coal—the optimum amount for an able-bodied stoker to handle.

As this more definitive approach to the analytical process in manufacturing took hold, men like Frank Gilbreth and Harry Gantt contributed to its growth. They, and others, instituted a methodology that took root in our industrialized society and became what is commonly referred to as industrial engineering.

Gilbreth developed the technique of breaking a job down to its smallest elements of work activity. He coined the word "therblig," in which each letter represents a work element, such as grasp, transport, inspect, and so forth. These early contributions to scientific management, which led to the development of time and motion study standards, served their industrial masters well during the heady days when industrial engineering made dramatic inroads into the archaic "seat-of-the-pants" approach to operating a factory.

In those days, industrial engineers swarmed over plant facilities like locusts, probing every conceivable weakness that might, through study, lead to increased labor productivity. They developed automated machinery, built tricky attachments, invented unique feeding devices, and used materials-handling equipment to synchronize the work flow. In addition, overhead cranes were integrated into the movement of production, and work simplification techniques were applied to further increase labor output. Even crusty Henry Ford put on an industrial engineer's hat when he initiated the assembly line to produce millions of Model T Fords.

Unquestionably, worker productivity did increase substantially during this golden era. But not all industrial engineers walked on water. There were some failures to offset the many successes and, indirectly, one of the debacles reflected on our old friend, Frederick Taylor.

According to an old-timer employed at the Acme Wire Company in Hamden, Connecticut, a group of industrial engineers known as the Taylor Boys was hired to install a production control system in the early 1930s. Production control was in its infancy in those days, and at Acme the function was handled by six general clerks tucked away in a small room adjacent to the plant superintendent's office.

The Taylor Boys made a management-consulting-type investigation and developed a new system. After they had explained the system to a skeptical works manager and to the plant superintendent, their plan was accepted and changes began to be made quickly. Deciding to keep only one of the six clerks, the efficiency experts neatly snipped five telephone wires during a lunch hour. When the five men whose phones were cut off returned from lunch, they got the message—they were fired!

Now the system was ready to go "on stream." The Taylor Boys had installed a myriad of interconnecting pneumatic tubes between each production department and production control to bring about the desired level of efficiency. Then they recruited "skilled" production control clerks to man the bastions in the new production control department. Since the system presumably would greatly increase productivity through better scheduling and machine loading, it was easy for the Taylor Boys to justify the employment of more clerks than before. Rows of cubicles were built to provide working space for these men.

The system boiled down to this: No work could be put on a machine without an authorization slip from a production control clerk. After an operation was completed, the foreman would sign off and return the slip to the production clerk via the tubes. The clerk would then determine the sequence for the operation to follow and shoot the instructions through the tube system to the next department

The system was quite complex and, as a result, some slippage in it began to occur. The Taylor Boys regarded this as only a temporary start-up problem and they plugged the dike by hiring more clerks. Things somehow went from bad to worse. Again, the solution was to add more clerks.

As the pieces of paper increased in volume with the full system in operation, the deluge became enormous. Since the average job required twelve operations, and there were about four hundred jobs in process at any given time, some five thousand work orders were constantly moving through those poor overworked pneumatic tubes. The clerks tried desperately to sequence the orders properly, but sometimes material wouldn't get to the machines when needed or there were unforeseen breakdowns, rejections, rework, and shortages. When these unexpected events occurred, all plans had to be changed immediately and the authorization slips redone.

Finally, the sheer weight of the whole mess forced the system to collapse. Work ground to a screeching halt on the production floor. The paperwork monster that would haunt modern man until the advent of the computer had turned on the master it was supposed to serve. The plant superintendent had had it; he stormed upstairs to the roomful of clerks—now numbering four times the original staff—and yelled, "Get the whole goddam bunch of these————out of here."

But progress in the field went on undaunted and industrial engineers continued to make great strides in the manufacturing area. Men such as Stagemerten, Mogensen, Maynard, and Barnes became prominent leaders in this recognized field of competence.

However, industry was becoming more complex and eventually required a broader overview than the industrial engineer could provide in his restricted environment. The old-time back-slapping salesman had given way to the person capable of understanding the full range of marketing, distribution, warehousing, and retail store management. The clerk in the back office had discarded his green eyeshade and was seeking accounting and financial know-how. The manufacturing department was no longer the place where the works manager was given a cash sum and allowed to disburse it as he saw fit. And engineers needed to become tuned in to the marketplace by designing a product for eye appeal, functional strength, packaging absorption characteristics, and ease of manufacturing.

It became virtually impossible for a business to survive under the autocratic dictates of a strong, lone individual. Specialists were springing up in a multitude of functional areas, and these men's developmental process required clearly defined job duties, technical training, and administrative guidance.

In the 1930s and mid-1940s, this trend toward specialization became evident to men such as Ed Booz, Carl Hamilton, and George Fry. They recognized a need in industry for people with expertise in various specialized areas. There was a further need for individuals who could apply this expertise through the use of scientific management methodology and industrial engineering techniques employed by their predecessors.

However, developing market recognition of a need for broad-gauged management consulting services was not all peaches and cream. While the industrial engineer could justify his wages by showing quantitative results through an increase in production, the consultant had to sell an intangible service that was extremely difficult to measure. Most of the emerging consulting skills were in staff or service-related organizational components rather than in basic line operations. Many of the early consulting assignments dealt with "people" problems. Also, the consultant's in-house counterpart usually lacked the experience and seasoning to contribute any added value to the assignment. As a result, there were many poorly defined, ill-advised, nonprofessional management consulting undertakings during this period of groping for identification and purpose.

Today, consultants straddle many fields of competence. They are knowledgeable in the broad categories of general management, marketing, manufacturing, procurement, personnel, packaging, research and development, administration, finance and accounting, and international operations.

Within these specialized skills, consultants may engage in a wide range of concentrated study and program applications. Among them are wage and salary administration, computer feasibility, corporate short- and long-range planning, turnaround, cost reduction, management audit, materials management, executive compensation, attitude survey, marketing and product research, cost accounting, value analysis, packaging design and structural testing, and short-interval scheduling.

In addition, there are numerous areas of expertise that either are of a peripheral nature or are newly emerging. They include minority group training and development, crime prevention, environmental control, nursing and medical care for the sick and indigent, equal employment opportunities for women, and plant safety brought about by the recently enacted Occupational Safety and Health Act.

In an effort to limit the dimensions of their field, management consultants are seeking recognition as a distinct professional group. There are now a number of recognized consulting associations devoted to upgrading the calibre of consultants—the Association of Consulting Management Engineers (ACME), the Association of Management Consultants (AMC), and the Society of Professional Management Consultants (SPMC). In 1970, certification of people in this profession was begun by members of the aforementioned groups who founded the Institute of Management Consultants (IMC). There are approximately 500 founding members of the Institute, and other consultants are being certified as their applications are received and processed.

The management consultant of the 1970s is as different from the mid-1940s type of consultant as the latter was from his early industrial engineering predecessor. Today, consultants are constantly stirring the pot with new ideas and advanced state-of-the-art industrial applications. They can effectively restructure a disjointed organizational body, slash costs to stave off the flow of red ink, or aid in the promotion and marketing of a new product. Consultants have developed expertise in many esoteric endeavors involving knowledge of operations research, linear programming, and computerized game theory techniques.

Consultants are a viable, dynamic part of the new technological explosion, and you better believe it! The Young Turks in business today are restive and eager to get action fast. If his corporation moves too slowly in adopting new techniques, then a Young Turk will get his accomplishment "kicks" by moving into consulting, where he can work with the full weight of authority from top management backing his recommendations. Consultants are expensive day workers, hired for a specific task and then released by the client at the completion of the assignment. But in most instances, they provide the least costly means of obtaining specialized assistance.

Furthermore, company managements receive another benefit from engaging consultants. It is the most important one. *While he is in their employ, they can pick the brains of the consultant for all the useful knowledge he possesses on a given subject. In fact, they would be foolish not to do so!*

The following chapters deal with my experiences as a management consultant.

1
Two Hats and a Hundred Hands

The train gradually picked up speed as it pulled out of the Massapequa, Long Island, station. I had begun what was to prove a fateful journey for me, for during the hour-long ride to New York City, my career in management consulting would begin.

I had just "hung up my shingle," and as the train clacked over the rails, I pondered how I would get started in this field. It was strange, I mused, that to be a consultant a person did not need a degree or certification. He need not have proven experience, or executive position in industry, or large capital investment. Yet, consulting is one of the highest-paying professions in the United States. The fee for many assignments runs to five figures, and some fees eventually reach the hundreds of thousands.

When a consultant submits a proposal to a client, his recommendations will rarely indicate specific dollar savings or other tangible benefits to be derived from this investment in his services. Few management consultants will put their reputations on the line by making firm commitments on the results they will achieve.

This reluctance is understandable, because the consultant is basically an advisor and, as such, he does not exercise authoritative control over the corporate environment. He is subject to many variables in the equation—corporate policy, attitudes of inside people, established procedures, entrenched work habits, degree of management acceptance of outside assistance, and the extent to which the complexities of a problem render the problem solvable.

Instead, the consultant will submit a thoughtfully defined proposal that covers the intended scope of the investigation, the objectives to be accomplished, the methodology to be employed, the number of man-days required, and the cost of these services.

As I gazed out the window on this bright, sunny morning in May, I reflected upon my past. My thoughts idled through my many years of industrial experience, from bench laborer and machinist to numerous staff and line positions, which had led eventually to executive posts with a number of blue chip companies. Among the benefits of this wide-ranging job experience was the frontline knowledge of how workers feel and act, which I had acquired through membership in a number of unions. In addition, I had sat as a representative for management on the other side of the bargaining table in hard-fought labor relations matters.

The train kept inching closer to New York City, each station bringing me nearer to that newly decorated office on Madison Avenue that would be home for my fledgling company

But how was I going to obtain my first client?

Suddenly, I heard my name mentioned and I was startled to see a neighborhood acquaintance, George Whiteside, sitting nearby. With the city still forty-nine minutes away, we struck up a conversation. At forty-four minutes to go, I mentioned to George that I had left the security of a multinational corporation to do consulting.

George seemed interested. As president of the Curtain Corporation of America, he had his share of headaches and his number one problem of the day was how to control production.

Sensing my willingness to open the matter up for discussion, he exclaimed, "Orders are being shipped late, back orders are mounting, customers are shouting for goods. And it is the height of the season and our inventories are in horrendous shape.''

I asked, ''Doesn't your production control system respond to these conditions, George?''

''Production control? Who ever heard of production control in the rag business? You're lucky if bundles of cuttings get through the plant without getting lost, let alone on schedule.''

I glanced at my watch—thirty minutes left to Penn Station in New York.

''Well, George, there are many workable methods and systems that can be used to chop this problem down to size,'' I replied. ''Order forms can be designed for multiple use, including internal follow-up tickets. Visual record cards are much faster for a clerk to scan than conventional inventory control records housed in a file. Factory work orders belong on preprinted ticket-a-graph equipment. These orders should be loaded into production using time-studied standards, or if you haven't standards, then with production actuals. And batch control of bundles will tighten the sequence of production lots in the plant and provide a feedback of data to complete the loop in the production control cycle.''

The train ride had sixteen minutes to go.

George had many questions to ask. I answered some of these queries with, ''Use color-coded bundle tickets to enable workers and supervisors to distinguish between different jobs. In fact, labor reporting can be tied right into the system in order to account for completed piece work.''

Ten minutes more and George would be heading for his curtain factory in a loft on East Twenty-third Street.

''Tell me, Jerry, what exactly can you do for me? How will it help me out? What will it cost? How long will it take?''

Five more minutes of riding time. My head was spinning. I wanted that first job!

''Five hundred dollars for five days' work,'' I replied. ''This will include a complete study of your plant operations—offices as well as factory—and a written report covering each recommendation in detail. Also, if you accept my proposals,

11

The train suddenly jerked to a stop. We had passed through the tunnel under the East River and had arrived at Penn Station. Time remaining: none.

"Jerry, you've got the job. When can you start?"

"George, if you want to get it done as soon as possible, how about right now?"

And so I began my career as a consultant.

Just as any other business, management consulting can be successful if one sells a quality product, at a competitive price, on time, and backed by reliable service. Sure, at the beginning I "worked my tail off" for less money, in order to establish myself. I needed the income but, more important, I wanted the referrals. My completed assignments had to sell my services–and that's the way it should be.

I had a good friend who had worked many years with a major consulting firm and then decided to strike out on his own.

He said to me, "Jerry, I learned the business well. There are three things you must do. Sell your services, control the operation, and do the job. Of these, the last is the least important." He stayed in business less than eight months.

That $500 fee from George Whiteside didn't last long, and soon I began to realize that days pass quickly when you sell your services on a per diem or job basis. So I had to do what I had been preaching to others—sit back and plan my business from a purely objective and dispassionate viewpoint.

First, this involved taking stock of my strengths and weaknesses. I had worked for many large firms: a leader in air conditioning, a multinational natural resource company, a major chemical and drug manufacturer, a prominent specialty steel producer, a national data processing supplier, and an aerospace products manufacturer. With this diversified experience, which had touched on most functional areas, I regarded myself to be best qualified to practice as a broad-gauged general management consultant rather than as a specialist. Since most consultants concentrate on a relatively confined area of expertise, I would be trading off less in-depth knowledge against greater proficiency in a wider range of client needs.

Next, I reviewed my academic training. Undergraduate and graduate degrees in business administration. Again, my background was diversified, with majors in sales management and industrial engineering, and minors in accounting and personnel administration. This was a solid base, since consultants, in general, lack consistency in formal education. Some have no academic qualifications, although most consultants hold degrees in business administration and liberal arts. A good percentage have advanced degrees, doctorates in the applied sciences, certification in public accounting, or legal bar acceptance.

My particular combination of industrial experience and formal training qualified me to handle assignments involving corporate turnarounds, clerical cost control, methods and work simplification, materials management, production planning and control, personnel administration, short- and long-range planning, policy formulation, and general management

Once I had established my company identity, I spent many hours at the nearby public library, searching for prospects in Standard and Poor's, Thomas Register, Moody's and Dun and Bradstreet. My strategy was to seek companies located within 200 miles of New York, in a field allied to my previous work experience, large enough in sales volume and number of employees to support the use of an outside consultant, yet not of the size requiring an extensive staff of in-house specialists.

Although my prior experience had been with large firms, I had yet to establish a track record as a consultant; so I avoided head-on competition with the full-service management consulting firms that concentrate on *Fortune* 500 companies.

Recognizing that the real world is highly competitive in any industry, I made a rough thumbnail appraisal of my competition as follows:

- *Large management consulting firm.* Bright, articulate people with academic training from the Harvard Business School, Stanford, Ivy League universities, or military academies. Upper fifth of class. Lacking heavy industrial experience, but capable of mastering the field under the tutelage of experienced partners.
- *Management services arm of major accounting firm.* More reserved, introverted personalities. Training from Wharton School of Finance, Pace Institute, University of Chicago, or other schools with heavy concentration in accounting and finance. Assignments professionally executed with thorough supportive documentation.
- *Research-oriented firm.* Technically trained scholars with advanced degrees in mathematics or the sciences. Think tank type, preferring to analyze more complex business problems in esoteric fields. Reports rely heavily upon the reader's ability to understand and absorb findings, rather than upon finite recommendations. Academic training at schools such as M.I.T., Duke, and Georgia Tech.
- *Regional speciality house.* Less formal academic training, geared more to the particular needs of the local business environment. Heavy concentration in industrial engineering, plant studies, materials management, and special industry and commercial applications.
- *Medium-sized or small specialty shop.* Education can range from members who are certified public accountants, attorneys, and holders of doctorates in a technical field, to those with no formal academic training. Qualifications are based primarily upon prior applied experience in a particular segment of industry, commerce, or government. Generally, strong in a narrowly defined area of expertise that is of an unusual or unique character, such as computer application, sales training, urban and minority problems, agribusiness, international operations, or economic studies.
- *Independent management consultant.* Education generally parallels specialty shops. Tends to have one basic strength

but, in time, becomes a generalist. Maintains strong long-term ties with clients. High acceptance with company personnel and executive management. Works with other consultants, on referral basis, when additional expertise is required.

As I grew more deeply involved in consulting, I became acquainted with others in the field, and I participated in the formation of a group composed solely of independent management consultants. I learned that most of these independents had come from well-established consulting firms and had taken "hip pocket" accounts with them. Some members confided to me that the way to survive was to obtain retainer business. I never mentioned my lowly $100 per diem charges after I found out that their fees were much higher.

But I did gain additional information about consulting from these fellow practitioners. Through a questionnaire survey of the group membership, I learned that the average independent management consultant billed only 60 percent of his time. The balance was spent in selling his services, and "downtime." By comparison, the larger firms billed about 80 percent of a man's time; however, most of them absorbed the costs of the time the partner spent obtaining business and the administrative overhead costs.

I also learned that most consultants rely heavily on client referrals and repeat business. New prospecting is done through direct mail solicitation, guest speaker appearances, participation at industry seminars and associations, and publication of articles in trade magazines and periodicals.

Over a period of months, I had managed to obtain additional consulting assignments with a camera equipment rental company, a children's party dress manufacturer, a sporting goods producer, a masonry supply house, and a combination laundry and dry-cleaning establishment.

Although each assignment went well, I was torn with inner doubts. How could I go into *any* company, in *any* industry, look the place over, and then, as if by some magical formula, solve its problems? Sooner or later, I reasoned, a set of circumstances would confront me that my experience and training could not handle. Then what happens to you, Jerry Fuchs, management consultant? Will your entry into the profession be exposed for all to see? Will you then face hard reality and go back to your niche in industry, forever forsaking the wild blue yonder of counseling others?

I made more telephone calls, sent out more letters, and had more luncheons with business acquaintances. But there still was not enough return in billings to equal the days spent in researching new prospects and selling my services. With my bankroll dropping rapidly, I told myself that I might be able to survive three more months, if I was lucky.

Then it happened! The idea struck me one day as I was sitting back and trying to solve my own problem of how to get business. Why not write case histories of my accomplishments and offer them free of charge? Although this approach had been used in the forms field, office equipment field, materials handling field, and others, management consultants either had never thought about doing it or didn't believe in giving their services away. But it was perfectly ethical (I checked with the association) and it could be a relatively inexpensive method of obtaining business.

I went through my files—both my consultant's files and my records from my industry days—and came up with thirteen studies I had made that had enough substance for case material. Thirteen was not a very lucky number, but the cases were all too good for me to discard any of them just to buck superstition. These studies cut across a broad spectrum of industrial problem areas where substantial cost savings and other benefits had been achieved.

My next step was to contact a small ad agency for assistance. The agency people liked the approach and agreed to package it for a nominal fee. Now the hard work began. I had to convert technical reports into case histories that would be factual and specific, but not boring. My objective was to appeal to a broad audience without being too general. I had to open the door without giving away the store.

Gradually, my plan took shape. The brochure we prepared began with a lead-in page describing the services offered by my company. This was followed by a summary of each case history, highlighting my accomplishments in each situation. One case told about a profit improvement program that contributed significantly to the turnaround of an old-line chemical company. Another told about a functional study that resulted in a hefty cost reduction at a medium-sized metals company. A production control system installed in a foundry had speeded deliveries, increased productivity, and lopped $35,000 off overhead. Each case history ran between ten and fifteen pages and contained all the blow-by-blow details. Tell people what you can do, Mr. Consultant! Merchandise your services!

The case histories were typed on masters and reproduced by offset process, then collated and stapled into individual jackets made up in four attractive colors: orange, green, yellow and blue. These sets were eventually inserted into heavy-duty, gray bond folders as a portfolio of executive case material. The folder had an imprinted hand holding a card, which would contain the name of the individual receiving the cases.

Time was critical. It took six weeks to get the entire package on stream, which included one pass on a dictaphone, one rough draft, and then the final copy. I worked around the clock to keep my little business alive while all this time the clock was ticking pennies away in my bank account. The entire promotion—ad agency and printing cost—came to about $4,000. My next step was to write a series of letters that would interest prospective clients.

Research indicated that a series of three letters—each with a slightly different message, but with a common thread throughout—spaced from seven to ten days apart, would pull the biggest response. The first letter contained a testimonial lead-in attesting to the savings achieved in the profit improvement program of a client firm. The other letters included similar "for instances" on various assignments. A return card accompanying each letter offered the cases "at no obligation whatsoever"; to receive them, the reader merely had to circle the ones he desired. Included with the letter was a preprinted sheet stating my credentials.

The replies started trickling in. The postman, with his postage-due return card, didn't know that his trip to my office on the eighth floor at 280 Madison Avenue was the high point of my day. Two cards were received, another one, then three more. All told, about eight cards arrived. That was more than four times the average for direct mail advertising. I made a phone call, set up an appointment, and at last had a chance to sell a new prospect on my services.

It worked! Through this and subsequent mailings business was obtained from such companies as Glamorene, Ceco Industries, Modern Carpet Sweeper, Crest Manufacturing, Sterling and Sterling Insurance, Certain-teed Products, and Revere Copper & Brass.

Every job was done to the client's specifications, on time, within the agreed-upon fee. The pendulum had shifted. At last I was on my way. Dust off that shingle, Jerry, and keep it up there where it belongs—where the whole wide world can see it! Finally, I had found the combination needed to survive in this rough-and-tumble business.

I now had "two hats and a hundred hands." When I put on my working "hat," which pinned me down on a client assignment, my selling "hat" could continue to solicit business via a hundred letters delivered by postal carrier. Now I could concentrate all my efforts on doing a professional job, knowing that at any time another batch of letters would generate more live prospects.

I still kept my other contacts, made plenty of telephone calls, and hustled to meetings and luncheons. But the cases were manna from heaven—they bought me time, the rarest commodity when one is selling a service on a per diem basis.

As I completed additional jobs, I became aware that there was more to consulting than technical proficiency. I began to recognize the strong impact that personalities can exert on an organization. The effect was particularly noticeable in the smaller, family-dominated enterprises. It meant that I needed a deeper understanding of the causative factors behind individuals' psychological and economic motivations. Sometimes it required probing the illogic of family members who were driving themselves to the brink of mental breakdowns when they seemingly possessed everything: cars, yachts, racehorses, artistic masterpieces, beautiful women, prestige, and power. And, as if to counterbalance these unhappy cases, there were the genuinely warm family situations with their precious moments of joy and humor.

Accordingly, I found myself more than a disinterested observer of these emotional happenings. Instead, my trained objectivity had to be tempered to accept the human element in the equation.

This seasoning process in my development as a management consultant began with an assignment involving a guy named Henry.

2
Made of Iron

"Henry!"

"Yes, mother, I'm coming."

That dialogue introduced me to the inner workings of a family-operated business. The company was a small manufacturer of storage lockers, carpet sweepers, and metal chests, located in one of the outlying communities along the north shore of Long Island.

As you walked into the spacious, somewhat garish reception room, your eyes immediately were attracted to an enormous bronze bust of the founder of the company who, according to the gold inscription, had departed from this earth and the Titan Carpet Sweeper Company ten years previously. But nothing had been changed by his fond son who had taken over as president.

Henry was now in his early fifties. He sat in a beautifully decorated, wood-paneled office located at the end of a forty-foot-long corridor. From the reception area to his private sanctuary, the hallway was dotted with open doorways leading into small offices where people engaged in typical home office clerical work: bookkeeping, billing, credit, order processing, and purchasing.

Back in the reception room, however, one person didn't conform to these nameless faces—the president's mother. As the wife of the founder, she was a formidable woman who had worked in the company (probably in the same spot) since it began some fifty-odd years ago. Sitting in this most strategic vantage point, she could—and did—screen all visitors, check most incoming calls, and review all of the company mail. In fact, she ran the company! When she had something to "discuss" with her son during the day, she would yell "Henry," and immediately he would appear at the doorway to his office awaiting her command.

After making a detailed analysis of the office systems and procedures, I completed my study, offering many time-saving ideas. Then I made one more suggestion to Henry—get rid of your mother!

Henry surprised me by accepting the challenge and, after further discussion, he agreed to talk Mama into taking a long, leisurely vacation in Europe.

With work kit in hand, I moved on to another assignment, temporarily losing contact with Henry. But as a true professional should, I returned a few weeks later for a follow-up visit. Henry looked and acted like a new man and the office staff seemed to be in a more buoyant mood.

"Things are working out very well," he said.

Mama had apparently accepted the inevitable. As Henry and I were talking, we were interrupted by his mother, who walked into his office to report that the morning mail had not been delivered because the mail girl was out sick, and to ask if she should handle this chore.

Henry said firmly, "No, that's not your job," and immediately assigned the task to someone else. "See," he exclaimed triumphantly (after his mother had departed), "Mama will no longer meddle; in fact, she should be ready to sail for Europe in a few weeks."

So I picked up my trusty attache case, stamped the file folder "completed," put on my hat and, with a firm handshake, strode out into the glorious sunshine.

Less than a year later, however, Henry sold the company. The reason was quite simple. His mother had managed to remain active and to continue her strong influence in the organization. Henry's better employees had resigned in total frustration. No sooner were well-defined systems and work procedures established than his mother intervened and insisted they be discarded. It was impossible to delegate tasks to subordinates without his mother's interfering presence being felt.

The old girl was made of iron—and was just too strong for Henry. It would have taken far more than a consultant (or all the king's men) to have made Henry the equal of his mother. Maybe the wrong person was on that pedestal in the reception area. Mama had a carload of intestinal fortitude—or "guts," as we say in the trade—and it was Henry, instead of his mother, who went to pasture.

As a management consultant, I had to go beyond basics and try to grasp the significance of Henry's frustrations. Behind my proposal to banish Henry's mother was the need not only for Henry to become a mature individual, but also for all the people in the company to be given an opportunity to assume responsibility with commensurate authority. The company was stagnating because of the stifling effect of the old gal, even though she had been largely responsible for its initial success.

Why is it that closely related individuals, who should be working in harmony, so often destroy one another in needless conflict? I've pondered this enigma, trying to find the answer to its seemingly odd contradiction. Does it somehow stem from the psyche of family relationships—father against son, brother against brother, Cain against Abel?

Each of the two owners of a major parachute manufacturing concern had a son working for the company. Both younger men were in their early thirties, intelligent, and well-educated. Both had more than ten years' experience in the firm, yet both held relatively insignificant jobs. This was not their own doing but reflected a lack of confidence on the part of their fathers, who ran the organization through intuitive feel.

The basic assignment given to me included establishing a data processing department; installing a production control system; labor reporting; setting up scrap and rework controls; introducing cost accounting procedures; and establishing labor incentives. But my final report didn't stop after covering the proposals on operating improvements—it stated strongly that the two sons were long overdue to assume some primary responsibility.

The controller had recently suffered a severe heart attack and was unable to continue in this position. Upon my recommendation, he was transferred to contract administration and one of the sons was promoted to the post of controller. The home office needed a competent purchasing agent and the other son fitted the job specifications perfectly. Both men soon became outstanding executives. If the fathers had been asked why they were unable to recognize their sons' abilities, they might have answered, "We couldn't see the forest for the trees."

Although members of a family frequently can be exasperating in a day-to-day working relationship, over the long haul they are often a company's strongest asset.

Soon after the assignment with the parachute company, I was retained by a small laundry in Center Moriches, Long Island, seventy miles east of New York City. The entire laundry operation consisted of five members of the controlling family and a handful of other employees. Peter Klechinski, the owner, handled the walk-in counter business. His wife, Jenina, supervised two girls and also did a solid day's work on flat ironing. The youngest son ran the wetwash operation, while two other sons took care of route deliveries.

At the beginning of the study, I expected to increase profits through conventional means such as machine loading, cost control, establishing production standards, and improving the work flow; but it soon became evident that the wealth of the company was in the talents and hard work of the family members. Therefore, I decided to mold my recommendations around these qualities.

I had obtained a population trend report from the Long Island Lighting Company, information from the local Chamber of Commerce, and a breakdown of previous sales. This data revealed that the county had been growing rapidly, and a considerable amount of overhead-absorption type business was available on a contract basis with hospitals, motels, summer resorts, and government installations. Mike, the eldest son, was placed in charge of institutional business, and within a few months he acquired a substantial amount of contract work.

Using maps of the area that showed population density, we were able to develop a marketing plan by dividing existing territories and expanding into adjacent geographic regions. Each realigned or new territory had sufficient potential to support another person. The second son was given responsibility for route sales and for establishing delivery salesmen's quotas and incentive pay. He immediately began to promote the highly profitable flatwork through a customer coupon offer. The sales curve shot up.

The youngest son, Tom, was relieved of his supervisory job in the wetwash department and was replaced there by an experienced worker. Tom then took over a newly formed dry-cleaning operation—which is the area where the best profits are to be found in that industry.

With each person pulling his weight, the company was soon working two shifts during the winter months and operating around the clock during the resort season. Klechinski's became the dominant laundry and dry-cleaning establishment in that area and grew strong enough financially to acquire its major competitor.

A consultant can prescribe the most modern management techniques, but in the final analysis the company must be willing to follow the prescription. At Klechinski's, the family recognized this and accepted the recommended changes in organization. In this instance, the family pulled together and the results showed it.

As the assignment came to an end, I received a special bonus in personal satisfaction when the boss's wife finally could afford to take time off for a well-deserved vacation.

As one can readily appreciate, family situations can be dangerous and difficult to resolve. Yet on occasion they are amusing. Rainette, a prominent women's raincoat manufacturer, had succeeded mainly through the aggressiveness and drive of the president, Dick Wolff. In the eight years since he had taken over the reins, company sales had skyrocketed from $2 million to $12 million. But he was a son-in-law and all the other executives were blood-related family: fathers, uncles, brothers, and sons.

Dick had retained my consulting services to engage in an overall front-office study. Yet each day he redefined the scope of the assignment as if he were unsure of the reason for hiring me. However, the problem soon became apparent—the infighting of the family was wearing his nerves thin and affecting his business decisions. Once I became aware of this situation, I concentrated my efforts on organizing accountabilities, responsibilities, and job definitions.

I spoke to Dick about establishing an executive vice-presidency, to be filled by a member of the family. It would neatlty bridge the existing delicate human relations gap. The best candidate for the spot, Dave Sherer, was heavy in the design, purchasing, and production areas, which counterbalanced the president's main interests in finance, general accounting, and front-office showroom.

Dick endorsed the plan and decided to hold a meeting the following night. His first call was to Uncle Hymie. While I listened to the telephone conversation, Dick explained the reason for the meeting. Suddenly, he roared like an enraged bull elephant and slammed down the receiver.

Before I could say, "What's the matter?", Dick started to sputter and spit out the cause of his outburst. "I'm the president of this company, but I can't have the meeting on Thursday because Uncle Hymie goes to art class that night—and he refuses to miss a session."

The meeting was held on the following Saturday, instead of Thursday, and the organizational plan was accepted. Yes, most families will fight and squabble sometimes. But one can overlook an Uncle Hymie's whims if sales and profits set new records year after year.

Although the consultant is usually an active participant in the changes that occur, in certain instances they are beyond his control. These changes may be the result of an "act of God," irreconcilable personality conflicts, irrational executive behavior, or a major shift in corporate policy. In some cases, the underlying cause of change may be a play for raw power or foolhardy bravado. But regardless of the reason, the outcome is the same—the consultant is in the unenviable position of bearing witness to the demise of a close business relationship.

Let's look at a few of these real-life vignettes, and reflect upon the action as it unfolds. Each company had been a client of mine. Perhaps if I had been given the opportunity to become intimately involved, I might have been able to influence the events that occurred; but more likely, the severe emotional and psychological complexities of these situations would have rendered the task virtually insurmountable.

The setting was the heyday of the darlings of Wall Street—the conglomerates. The year was 1968. But it was a tragic period for Werner Engel, president of Universal Camera Equipment Corporation. Werner had devoted his life to building up Universal and had finally been able to retire after turning the business over to his son.

Allen Engel had been a dashing bachelor who preferred to roam, rather than work at a nine-to-five job. But as his father grew older, it became necessary for Allen to settle down; he married a lovely Swedish blonde and became vice-president and heir apparent. Soon Allen had a family, and Werner could begin to feel assured that the business was in safe hands. Unfortunately, fate had other plans.

Allen was offered a trip to Europe by one of the firm's customers—a producer who rented cameras, rigs, lighting equipment, and Moviola editing machines for his films. Allen and his wife boarded an overseas flight for a week of fun and frolic. Over the Atlantic, the plane was caught in a fierce storm and disappeared without a trace of any survivors.

Werner was forced back from retirement, but for some time he was unable to comprehend the tragedy that had happened to him. He couldn't believe that his son was gone. Ironically, a sign painter had just begun to letter Allen's name on the door of a new executive office. Werner refused to stop the worker from his task and insisted that his son would be found alive.

The news spread rapidly to Wall Street—the old man, broken and bowed, finally wanted to sell the business in order to settle his son's estate. Universal was snatched up by a mini-conglomerate low on cash, but with enough borrowing power to buy out Werner's company at a depressed valuation. His loyal employees tried desperately to purchase the company with limited funds and a promissory note for the balance, but Werner wanted out.

The conglomerate was in electronics, avionics, medical supplies, and other street-name "hot" companies. Soon, cash and liquid assets were being siphoned off from Universal to feed the insatiable appetite of the parent company and its other subsidiaries. Then the market collapsed in the debacle of 1970–1971, and with it went the parent company and Universal. Yes, on the way down the directors tried to salvage what remained. But, the effort was to no avail, for Universal had really died three years earlier—in a plane lost off the coast of Ireland.

Mavericks usually gravitate toward the smaller, entrepreneurial type firms, while the organization men seek employment with the big-name companies. However, there are some mavericks still in the corporate fold—until they are discovered, that is.

Hank Folsom was an overly aggressive executive with the FPC Company, a manufacturer of automobile supplies, who had a propensity for demanding the impossible of his subordinates. After the third turnover of virtually his entire staff, the president of FPC, Frank Browning, decided that Hank should undergo sensitivity training in California. The sessions were conducted by a management consulting firm that specialized in this field. Hank was summoned to the home office for a man-to-man chat. Browning told him about the program and how it would help him overcome his apparent hostility to other people.

"Hank, I know this sensitivity training will be good for you. It's been tried by many companies to improve a person's relationship with others in the corporate environment. Granted, it's still new for industry, but there have been a number of successes to date. It involves stripping yourself nude in the presence of others and communicating freely with them. In doing this, you are able to purge yourself of these latent, hostile feelings."

Hank left the president's office and headed back to his $150,000 home in Short Hills, New Jersey. Could he undergo this apparent degradation and loss of identity? Did he really want to alter his personality and subvert the drive and aggressiveness that had propelled him to a high-level executive position?

Hank had one hour and ten minutes to think about the sensitivity training program that Browning had outlined to him.

He pulled into his driveway at 3:30 P.M. with his mind made up. He never went back—the president received his resignation in the morning mail.

Farrington Steel is located in the Shenandoah Valley region of West Virginia, between the Blue Ridge and the Allegheny mountains. It is the dominant company in a small, inbred community. The present owners are fourth generation Farringtons. All employees attend the Grace Episcopal Church each Sunday because directly across the street a dedicated employee "ticks off" the names on a weatherbeaten ruled sheet as they enter the front door.

All executives, from middle management up, are expected to live in the company town. They are also encouraged to observe their ranking in the organizational hierarchy by purchasing a home at an appropriate level on the side of the surrounding mountain.

I had done a number of consulting jobs at Farrington and recognized the rigidity imposed upon the community by the controlling family. People who worked for Farrington had to be willing to accept conformity and togetherness. In return, the company offered a blend of paternalism and security that was very tempting. Mavericks don't go within one hundred miles of this type of company. If they joined one, by accident rather than design, it would be a short-term relationship.

I had been away working on another assignment when Tom Harper was interviewed and hired as the assistant general manager of Farrington, to be an eventual replacement for the general manager, who had Parkinson's disease. The choice of Tom for that position was a mistake, and if I had been at the plant at the time, I would have voiced my objections. The chemistry wasn't there. One of the most important skills that a consultant develops is the ability to evaluate the corporate personality and make the proper fit between the organization and the person. Tom was too urbane, sophisticated, and strong-willed to fit into the Farrington environment.

The stifling influence of the community soon affected Tom's attitude toward the job. In frustration, he demanded to take over as general manager immediately, even though his superior's health had stabilized. Tom lost his bid and was severed from Farrington. He knew it would happen—only the timing was uncertain.

You couldn't have found two men farther apart in temperament and personality than Carl and Max. Yet, they were partners in Supreme Products, a highly successful import-export company.

Their economic road to fortune began in a crowded storefront on East Tenth Street in New York City. Shortly after the end of World War II, both men had gone there to bid on army surplus goods. Each had about $500 to spend on rafts, K-rations, tool kits, and Mae West life preservers. Somehow they started talking to one another and, on the spot, decided to pool their meager resources. That was the start of Supreme, which, by 1969, was a $4 million import company with offices and warehouses in New York, Houston, and San Francisco.

But something had gone wrong during these growth years. The accountant who brought me into this assignment had said, "Jerry, I had them in my office on a business matter and words started to get heated. It was so bad that I had to physically stop them from coming to blows."

The actual straw that had broken the camel's back and caused this dangerous situation was an innocent little IBM 6400 machine. It is a specialized unit that handles inventory, receivables, and billing in one operation. After shipment is made, the operator pulls a magnetic-coded receivables card from a tray and automatically transfers the heading information on the card to an in-line printer for entry of data on sets of continuous invoice forms.

After this operation, each inventory item card is withdrawn from a housing unit inserted in the machine and the data are punched directly on the card. The card is automatically updated to reflect the withdrawal from stock and the new balance on hand. After all items have been posted to each inventory card and simultaneously to the invoice with automatic line extensions, the totals are computed (with freight and parcel post handled on separate cards) and the invoice is completed.

Although the complete operation is a rather slow process, the machine does offer the advantage of immediate inventory posting and billing—a critical operation at Supreme, with its volume of over two hundred invoices per day and an average of ten to fifteen line items on each invoice. Max had put the machine into use and fought to keep it; Carl thought the $1,200 monthly rental charge was excessive. The machine also required two operators working continually through the lunch hour and overtime to handle the volume. With additional programming, the machine had the capability to store an entire day's shipments and furnish daily reports on dollars shipped by product group.

I was asked to evaluate the justification for the machine and improve general office efficiency. It was not an easy assignment because communications between the two partners had broken down completely–neither was talking to the other.

Carl was a tall, erect urbanite of German extraction, in his late fifties. An actor in his youth, he enjoyed using flourishes and gestures from the Wagnerian school to make a point. Childless, he and his wife enjoyed the good things in life—operas, shows, choice cuisine, intimate parties with close friends, and occasional trips to Europe. While Carl being in his late fifties, had slowed down appreciably, Max, a junior by fifteen years, was still as fiery and volcanic as ever. A family man living in the suburbs, Max divided his energies "equally" between business and family: 90 percent for business, 10 percent for his family. The company consumed all his enormous energy and drive, and he wanted the business to continue to grow.

It was only my second day at Supreme when Carl "invited" me to join him in the showroom to listen to his problems. Attempting to play the role of an industrial psychologist, I sat back in one of the oversized leather reclining chairs and listened to the flashbacks of Carl's unhappy relationship with his partner. He gave me a blow-by-blow, systematic dissertation on the countless errors in judgment that Max had made and the cost to the company of each error.

The next day it was Max's turn: he cornered me in the basement stockroom and gave his version of the difficulties he had with Carl. At one point in this mental Ping-Pong game, I suggested to Carl that he try to learn more about his partner by offering to have a few drinks with him at a nearby cocktail lounge. Carl reared back on his hind legs, stared me down from his rigid six-foot–two-inch height, and said, "Jerry, you want *me* to go to a *bar*?"

I responded with, "Not a bar, a cocktail lounge," and let it go at that.

My report was finally completed, and I arranged to meet with the partners in one of their extra offices. The outside accountant was also present. The meeting began with good rapport and seemed to be holding steady; in fact, everything was going smoothly until the IBM machine justification came up.

I had recommended keeping the machine because it could provide automatic updating of inventory as each item transaction on the invoice was posted. Also, at the end of each day, or week, the machine could furnish analytical data of shipments made to customers. I supported my conclusions with figures showing that yearly inventory savings could cover the rental charges of the machine and payroll reductions could generate additional cost savings.

However, at this point in my presentation, Carl rose from his seat, slowly paced the office, and in his deepest and most resonant voice began to needle the daylights out of little Maxie.

Max jumped to his feet and rushed toward Carl in an outburst of frustration and anger. Again, a meeting between the two partners had almost ended in blows and it had not resolved some of their management concerns, such as the fate of the IBM 6400.

However, there was one recommendation in the report that I felt might possibly save the business. I had stated that, until they could reconcile their differences, a five-man steering committee should be established to run the company. It would consist of three outside members plus the two partners. "Otherwise," I said, "get a divorce and sell the company."

Three weeks went by before my phone rang. The call was from Max. "We like the steering committee idea and agree it's our only hope," he said. "But we don't want the odd man who could swing the vote against us. Instead, we want to set it up with just four men. Each of us is to propose two men. The other partner will then select the one he prefers. I would like you to be one of my two choices."

I agreed, and after finding out that the old 6400 was still

perking—and producing invoices better than ever—I ended the conversation on a friendly note.

Less than a week later, I received another call from Max. "Sorry, Jerry, but Carl took the other fellow."

Because the committee was, after all, my suggestion, curiosity and pride impelled me to call Carl to find out why he had not chosen me. "Jerry," he said, "please don't take this personally. You're a fine person and I like you very much. But I picked the other man because he's a psychiatrist at Columbia University. I want him on the committee because *I think my partner is nuts.*"

So, after a strategic withdrawal, I went back to amateur headshrinking status.

The steering committee did work, and eventually Carl and Max learned to adjust to one another's personality quirks. The business prospered, policy decisions were made, and actions were taken; but the changes were not accomplished overnight!

Maybe American businessmen are nuts! Is there a more disproportionate percentage of paranoid schizophrenics in our society than in otthers? If so, excluding "career" executives for the moment, can it be because the second generation son who inherits the mantle from his father is castrated and defrocked?

In African tribes (and most primitive cultures), when a boy reaches puberty he is given a spear and scant rations and is sent off to fend for himself in the jungle before being accepted into manhood. He must go out and either kill the lion or be killed himself.

We hand our sons dead carcasses and thereby deprive them of the opportunity to prove any semblance of manhood. Before we even advance them to the executive suite, they must endure years of torment and degradation. Is it any wonder that these men, when given the ultimate assignment, *must* prove themselves in order to satisfy a strong guilt complex? The method is simple: each one says, "First, I'll become a

33

millionaire, and then I'll build the business to a height that will be my everlasting monument, and mine alone."

To satisfy this lust for power and recognition, he must flagellate his subordinates into submission. Only then does he seem to reach full gratification for the role that life has dealt him.

3
From Little Acorns Grow Mighty Oaks— Sometimes!

The United States, with its capital formation economic system and tremendous wealth of natural resources, produces a race of rugged entrepreneurs. These individuals are unlike the majority of U.S. citizens and are different from their counterparts in other areas of the globe. Bold, imaginative, aggressive, and technically competent, they strive for success as though it were the elusive morning star—ever in sight but never to be held. Constant frustrations and demanding pressures are their lot. But for these adventurers of commerce and industry, having their own business is an overriding and compelling passion.

Although each individual is stamped with his own unique personality characteristics, young and ambitious Andrew Carnegie, after his arrival in Pittsburgh in 1887, became a composite of their mold. After rising to become division superintendent of the Pennsylvania Railroad Company, he sensed the need for railroad steel and entered the steel business in the early sixties. From that time on, entrepreneur Carnegie went into railway manufacture—car axles, railway bridges, pig iron, Bessemer steel, open-hearth steel. He owned an ore-hauling railroad, a fleet of ore boats, and ore lands. Finally, in the 1890s, he reorganized the whole disparate mixture of his industrial empire into a closely knit, compact, corporate entity.

Learning from Carnegie's success, a youthful and poised Charles M. Schwab presented the concept of a vertically integrated steel company to J. P. Morgan, the financial wizard, in a Pittsburgh hotel room. Schwab envisioned a company that was fully integrated, from the mining of the raw materials (iron ore, coal, and limestone) through the smelting of the iron from the ore and its refining into steel; to the shaping of the steel into finished products such as rails, pipes, wire, and nails, and into semifinished products such as steel plates, sheets, and bars.

Morgan accepted the concept and financed the organizational structuring of the United States Steel Company. Eventually, disagreements developed, and entrepreneur Schwab moved on to establish the second largest company in the industry—Bethlehem Steel.

When William C. Durant formed General Motors through the acquisition and consolidation of about two dozen existing companies, he carried out a revolutionary plan that could only have succeeded through the entrepreneurial flare of a man with his exceptional promotional genius. But since he lacked administrative talent, Durant was eventually forced to relinquish control of the company, and he died in poverty and relative obscurity.

A company's origin can be traced to an inventor of a new product or process, a promoter of an idea, or a merchandiser with a different approach to reaching the consumer. King Gillette made his fortune by replacing the strop razor with a disposable, double-edged safety razor blade in a holder. Wanamaker, the merchant prince, who first sold his wares from a pushcart, made his mark when he moved to a fixed location from which he could exploit his merchandising talents. The partnership team of Sears and Roebuck recognized how inaccessible the marketplace was for the farmer and so developed the mail order catalog business to satisfy the farmer's needs.

Most companies follow an evolutionary pattern that moves through four distinct stages: promotional and developmental, production, marketing, and financial.

In the first stage, the company is formed by a person who has developed a new product or process, or has an idea that has certain unusual characteristics. At the second stage, investment capital must be obtained to build plant facilities, or to procure merchandise, and the product must be manufactured or made available to the consumer.

At the marketing stage, the company endeavors to make the consumer aware that the product exists and has value for him. The last stage of the cycle involves financial management and control, which is necessary in order to ensure that the company will remain solvent and fiscally sound. These stages become the basic functions needed to sustain an on-going business enterprise.

At its inception, and during its life cycle, the business will require an infusion of capital. Money can be acquired in several ways: through debt financing, equity participation, cash flow regeneration, personal investment, or borrowing.

There are many sources available to the businessman for borrowing seed money or additional funds—commercial banks; insurance companies; venture capital corporations; factors; government-affiliated operations such as the Small Business Administration, SBICs, and MESBICs; or individual investors.

Each method of financing has its advantages and disadvantages. Commercial banks tend to be more conservative, lending money against proven accomplishments and sound expectations. Other lending institutions charge a higher interest rate for the use of money. Some allow the entrepreneur to retain complete ownership, while others may dilute his equity through sweeteners such as warrants, options, conversion privileges, or other "kickers."

The stakes are high in the game of getting started in business. There are treacherous undercurrents of strategies and intrigue that can pull an unwary businessman down through a corporate takeover coup, or loss of effective operating control. Each situation is different; and it is precisely the uncertainty of the outcome that makes the game so inviting to those who enjoy pitting their wits against another person's will.

Management consultants are frequently engaged to participate in the formation of a new business venture. This may involve use of their expertise in the areas of finance, marketing, or new product development—or in putting together the entire package.

The consultant, through exposure of many varying situations, can discern certain directional paths that most ventures tend to follow. Although these paths are often obscured because of the personalities involved, the uniqueness of the product, an inability to pinpoint the precise market, or other complex factors, nevertheless, they are discernible to the trained observer. Therefore, in a representative sampling of case histories, the consultant can find common threads having general application. On this premise, let's view the following occurrences from the vantage point of the consultant and thereby gain greater insight into, and better understanding of, the ways in which people try to get started in business.

Fisherman's Wharf would have been the most beautiful marina in the world. It would have faced the picturesque Palisades. At night the view would have been breathtaking—a panorama of lights from the George Washington Bridge to the skyline of New York, amid the twinkling headlights of cars speeding along the Henry Hudson Parkway. But Fisherman's Wharf never made it—and none of the people in New York City ever knew what was happening.

Like most new businesses, Fisherman's Wharf started with an idea. It was Les Ward, the district sales manager for a national liquor distillery who saw its potential. As he drove to work, Les used to pass the pier at 125th Street where the Hudson River Day Liners formerly picked up passengers on their way up the Hudson River to Albany. Once the pier had bustled with activity. Now it stood empty and unused—a victim of changing times—for the day liner service had been cancelled.

One day, as Les Ward drove to his Harlem territory, he saw the pier in an entirely different light. Why not make it the hub of a marina? The pier could be rebuilt to house a rooftop restaurant, a cocktail lounge, a yacht agency, a yacht supply store, a marine training school, and other related enterprises. There was ample space for slips to berth 500 pleasure boats comfortably. With its location at the midpoint of Manhattan Island, the marina could satisfy the needs of scores of boat lovers living in and around New York, as well as the many transients visiting the city. And that glorious view at night would make Fisherman's Wharf the mecca for late diners and social imbibers.

Les needed help to promote his idea. Through various contacts, he soon assembled a promotion group consisting of a state senator, two local businessmen, and a public relations consultant. Les was aware that when you are dealing with a government body, you should have a political affiliation as well as participation by members of the business community.

Next, he began to make overtures to the New York City agency that controlled land of this type—the department of marine and aviation. Months passed and Les was now deeply involved in the plan at the conceptual level, the first step in a new venture. This involved determining the type of corporation to structure, the method of obtaining initial capital, the size of the marina, the mix of affiliated marina services, and the skills required to operate the business successfully.

At last, the complete venture package was assembled. It included a rendering of the marina with yachts bobbing at their moorings, the pier jutting out 200 feet into the smooth flowing waters of the Hudson, with the rooftop restaurant and cocktail lounge supporting the boldly printed letters, "Fisherman's Wharf—Welcome all ye weary travellers."

Les needed a financial report to present to the commissioner of marine and aviation. I prepared the study, breaking down the operation into two separate, independently supportable corporations—the marina, and the pier concessions and rentals. These figures had to be realistic to satisfy the demanding standards of lending institutions or venture capital corporations which would scrutinize the numbers to determine if they conformed to the concept.

First, the financial requirements were tailored to get the business going on a modest scale—enough to achieve the operating economies which the marina needed to be profitable. Then, after the company had consolidated its position, it could expand. This two-step approach would minimize the risks of a new business venture and enormously simplify financing.

A cash projection was made to determine how the money would be applied—that is, to what purpose and on what time schedule; and how the money would turn over—from what mix of Fisherman's Wharf boatmen and marina services the business would derive its income. The cash projection was then used to determine the payment schedule of fixed assets, payroll expenses, other operating needs, and cash flow. From this, I was able to develop a pro forma profit and loss statement and a pro forma balance sheet.

In addition to calculating the amount of money needed for the business, it was equally important to determine how the money would be used. Money going into the marina and pier facility would be fixed capital and, therefore, would come from stock and long-term loans. Short-term working capital would be needed to keep the business going and meet current cash demands.

The next step was to figure out how the money would be raised, the securities that would be offered to the investors, and the sources of funds. Many considerations entered into this judicious balancing of various options, such as which financial structure would be most profitable, which would best provide for future contingencies, which would best satisfy long-term corporate needs, and which would be most advantageous taxwise. Of course, any decision was largely dependent upon the availability of money and the terms upon which it could be obtained.

The financial decision was to trade on equity. This meant that Fisherman's Wharf would be formed with the least amount of equity investment and the highest possible proportion of debt financing. We recognized that this approach required maintaining earnings to meet interest payments or being subject to pressure by creditors. From the investor's standpoint, a thin capital structure offered the opportunity to accrue capital gains, which need not be taxed until realized and, when realized, are taxed more favorably than are dividends.

The final financial figures were ground out and they looked great. There was enough potential profit to attract a horde of investors, principally doctors, dentists, and small businessmen. Just think, here was a chance to make money in a legitimate business and each "partner" could have a sea captain's hat, complete with all the scrambled eggs. How could the promotion group miss!

The meeting with the commissioner of marine and aviation took place at 9:00 A.M. on a bright and cheery Wednesday morning. *We were TKO'd in exactly six minutes and twenty-two seconds.*

The omnipotent commissioner began by saying, "Gentlemen, I don't want to throw cold water on your proposal but, to safeguard the interests of the people of our city, I must insist on two conditions. First, the architectural firm doing the design work must be selected by the Commission and, second, all of the investors must meet our approval."

Pies are round and juicy. You can cut pies into eight, twelve, or even sixteen pieces. But like everything else in our finite world, pies can be divided into only so many parts. Fisherman's Wharf gurgled and sank out of existence three months later.

Les Ward's dream had vanished, yet there was a tragi-comedy sequel to the story.

Months later, the pier caught on fire. Les just happened to be nearby. As the firemen battled the blaze, chopping away at the wooden hulk, Les ran down to its smoldering edge and exclaimed loudly, "Stop, you're destroying *my* pier!

Boatmen leave New York City on weekends to recharge their emotional and physical batteries and breathe in some fresh air. Those unfortunates remaining in the city must somehow survive the weekend and be ready to do battle again the following Monday morning. More than three hundred cities in the United States have serious air pollution. Smoke, dust, fumes, radioactive wastes, odors, gases, and other contaminants burn and sear the inhabitants' eyes, eventually destroying their lungs, hearts, and bodies. Gasoline exhaust fumes account for most of the air pollution problem.

Companies are constantly searching for a method of controlling car emissions to combat this enemy of the urban centers. One man actually invented an antismog carbureting device back in 1958—and it worked. Yet the company never got off the ground

Chester Garvey, the inventor, was a construction engineer, pioneer pilot, plane and boat designer, and former head of the aeronautics department of the University of Miami. The device on which he received patent approval on July 4, 1961, was patent number 2,990,913 which replaced a standard carburetor on any truck or automobile engine.

Garvey's idea was ingenious. In layman's terms it can be explained in this way. If you were to throw a pint of gasoline on a hot pavement, you would expect to see the gasoline fumes rise. These fumes are the most volatile part of gasoline. The additives put into gasoline, such as varnish and carbon, are the dregs or heavy residue and do not burn off. Additives are put into gasoline to slow down the burning process. This is why additives serve the purpose of eliminating the "ping" in the engine. Pure gasoline (the first cracking of gas in the refinery), by contrast, would evaporate completely.

Chester Garvey's device blew a stream of air across a large area (or surface), creating a *fume*. By contrast, existing carburetors create a *vapor*. Since the fume is the cleanest and most volatile portion of the gasoline mixture, Garvey's device achieved virtually complete antismog combustion.

Heat is energy. When the tailpipe of a car becomes hot, the engine is releasing unburned hydrocarbons or wasted energy.

Chester Garvey and three other promoters set up a company to make this device. About one hundred small investors bought one-quarter shares, one-half shares, and a few whole shares apiece to finance the development of this new carburetion device. After two years, Garvey had a working prototype. It ran for hours without heat loss. You could hold the tailpipe hours after continual idling, and it was still at normal temperature. They tested it in a laboratory and found that virtually all carbon monoxide was removed. Most other contaminants were reduced sharply. The device produced complete combustion in the chamber—no raw gas went into the piston.

One brave advocate participated in a nonscientific test and survived. He sat in a car equipped with the new carburetion device. The car windows were closed, a rubber hose was attached from the tailpipe to a car window, and the engine was started. After four hours, he was unaffected by carbon monoxide fumes, and he experienced no adverse reaction.

A patent search was made and Chester Garvey's patent was first in line, with no others in contention. Now at last, members of "Cliff Dwellers Anonymous" had a knight in shining armor ready to slay that dreadful dragon—air pollution.

Then Garvey died suddenly and, through bungling and mismanagement, the company disintegrated and the prototype was inadvertently lost. However, it takes time to destroy an idea and a company. Four years went by before an action committee was formed to attempt to salvage the venture. The company had no funds and nothing to sell. It did have the patent, but other companies contacted as potential partners insisted that further developmental work would be needed before they would be interested in the device. Automobile manufacturers also wanted something more tangible before they would consider it. The situation was analogous to that ironic axiom that "banks will lend you money if you show sufficient proof that you don't need any."

The action committee contacted me and related the entire story. These small investors were hurting—some had invested $5,000 to $10,000 in a defunct enterprise.

"Jerry," they said, "we need an infusion of some more

dollars. A couple of hundred thousand dollars could redo the development effort and hopefully turn out a working prototype. But to interest prospective investors, we need a professional report that will sell 'the sizzle,' not the steak."

A stockholders' meeting was held, and I made a presentation. I told them quite frankly that my study was a long shot and it might not be successful. The vote was overwhelmingly to go ahead.

Setting the wheels in motion, I decided to lay the groundwork for replacing the prototype model in conjunction with making my study. Chester Garvey's tool and die maker, Bill Peters, had moved to Warren, Ohio. I flew out to meet with him, and he confirmed that, with his knowledge of the parts and assembly, he could reconstruct the unit. Furthermore, he was certain that his boss would allow him to use the machine tools in his plant to do this work after hours.

Next, I continued my journey to Phoenix, Arizona, to visit Mrs. Garvey. Members of the action committee had told me that Chester Garvey kept a little black book containing all his notations on the prototype. In my meeting with Mrs. Garvey, I explained my mission and asked about the notebook. She did have it and, after checking with her attorney, agreed to give it to us.

My last stop was in Los Angeles, California, where I visited a retired inventor and personal friend, Tom Farnsworth. After I showed him the patent and Chester Garvey's notes, and explained in detail how the carburetion device functioned, Tom became very interested in its potential application. On a handshake basis, he agreed to join the project as a consultant. In this capacity, he would work closely with Bill Peters on any necessary modifications in design and in the preparation of specifications and blueprints.

I then returned to New York with the nucleus of a team and new-found technical data that could be used to develop the prototype model.

My next step was to contact companies in the carburetor after-market. It was my intention to seek a joint venture, and it seemed that companies in this segment of the market would be more amenable to a proposition of this type than the original equipment manufacturers. By the time the study was completed, serious negotiations were in progress with one of these firms.

Agencies of various federal, state, and local governments were solicited for information on any antipollution laws and regulations. In certain instances, such as New York City, funds had to be approved for municipal support in any research efforts on devices of this type, although agencies were prohibited by law from engaging in the development of the final products. This wealth of data reflecting current government concern about pollution would play an important role in the documentation and conclusions reached by the study.

Finally, I compiled figures on unit and dollar volume sales, by market segment; projected unit costs of the antipollution device; cash flow requirements; projected capital requirements for machine tools and plant facilities; time-phased research and development payroll and other expense budgets; and the breakeven point when profits from the venture would equal start-up costs.

The study was completed with full documentation on the legal status of the patent, the capability to redevelop a prototype model, joint-venture interest, public need and possible research funding, and the market potential for the device. It was packaged with plenty of sex appeal, and combined with all of this substantive factual material. Investors were and still are interested—so are numerous underwriters.

At this writing, the project is still a long shot. Wall Street and "smart money" ask many probing questions before making a commitment. Only the small investors buy shares in untried companies. Perhaps if each person in New York City contributed two cents, Chester Garvey's carburetion device could be completed and placed in production. But what would the cliff dwellers complain about if they had no pollution problem, and had also won the daily double of venture capital, with a spanking new marina to boot?

Many industries play a role in making New York the conglomerate city that it is. Wall Street has made it the financial capital of the world; it is also the leading jewelry center in the United States; and the garment district adjacent to Seventh Avenue (or Fashion Avenue, as the street signs now proudly proclaim) sets the styles for the nation.

Next to the farmer, the soft goods manufacturer is the biggest gambler in the world. Style is king! A great line one year can bomb out the next. Whims and fancies of the unpredictable public make the business the biggest floating crap game alive. The average life expectancy of soft goods companies is seven years—and you could probably shave that statistic in half if you eliminated the third- and fourth-generation concerns whose founding fathers were farsighted enough to invest excess profits in Manhattan real estate and land in the suburbs. Their children, the grandchildren, and all the in-laws can survive a long time on papa's frugal ways and his monthly payment tenants.

It's a rough, tough, slug-it-out business with only a breather between the spring, fall, and holiday seasons. Usually the smart manufacturer hedges his bet by having one hundred or so bread-and-butter numbers. These are cut first and can be counted on to bring in a steady volume of orders. The balance of the line is cut in anticipation of what the smart buyers will select. Most of this buying frenzy reaches its vortex at the New York, Chicago, and West Coast shows. If you bomb out of these, count it as a blessing. Later on, you will have hocked the family jewels with a factor; and all your cars, your home in the suburbs, the mistress's flat, and the college education money will be tied up in inventory.

Should you survive this ordeal, and sell enough merchandise to stay in business and make a reasonable profit, you will also be entitled to a vacation in Miami Beach or Puerto Rico. But while your wife lolls in the sun in that new Rudi Gernreich bathing suit, better start thinking about next season's line because, like all your competitors, you're already one month behind!

Bob Diamond had been in soft goods for many years when he became a business fatality. And for two years or so, Bob was "on the beach"—or in semiretirement, if you were a friend and had asked the question.

Bob couldn't get back to the gaming table because he no longer had table stakes. So he worked at another job while waiting for an opportunity to arise. The chance came when a friend mentioned that he was interested in expanding his company by adding a sportswear division. The friend's large soft goods corporation realized that a demand existed in the children's wear field for a quality sportswear operation, and it wanted to expand in that direction.

Bob called my office and invited me to lunch. He had been very despondent since losing his company and said, "Jerry, I feel at times like jumping off the Brooklyn Bridge. I can't believe that I have no value to anyone."

Then he told me that he had this opportunity but needed some help in putting a proposal together. He also knew a fellow named Lou Morton whom he wanted to bring in as the sales manager.

The three of us got together and worked up a complete presentation on setting up a sportswear division. The product line was broken down into the spring, fall, and holiday seasons, then subdivided into boys' and girls' shirts and slacks and various sizes and ranges. We made marketing forecasts of these product lines to develop sales volume figures. The total number of styles of the initial line was estimated at approximately seventy to seventy-five samples, broken down into the various garment components—fabric embroidery, trim, and notions.

Various methods of distribution were analyzed to determine the advantages and disadvantages of using the existing company sales force, establishing a new sales force, or a combination of both, coordinated by the corporate sales manager.

Organization and personnel requirements for all executive and key personnel were drawn up to determine the type of people required and the estimated payroll costs.

47

Manufacturing facilities needed to establish this new division consisted of cutting tables, cutting machines, cloth spreader, overlocks, single needle sewing machines, special sewing machines, button sewers, and various shelves, bins, and other miscellaneous items. The manufacturing facilities were planned to handle the volume of production required by the market forecast.

The product line was analyzed and a cost table prepared showing the indicated markup in cost per dozen and wholesale price. This table provided figures based on a 38 percent markup which was the median in better retail store outlet pricing structure.

Pro forma statements were developed for a five-year period showing projected income and balance sheet amounts for each year and the payoff on return on investment for the business venture.

Bob and I then prepared a detailed time schedule indicating the specific steps required to bring the line out in time for the coming fall season. This schedule covered such things as organizing the sales force; selecting material and trim for the initial sample line; providing all designs and fabrics required; hiring key personnel; ordering fabrics for the sample line; duplicating the sample line; having the lines pinned, assembled, and shipped to the salesmen; ordering print tickets and logos; and other critical long lead time items.

The company liked this well-thought-out plan and established the new division. Bob made it work, and he is now back on top of the heap. There is talk around town that the Brooklyn Bridge will soon be junked. Bob couldn't care less— he always was afraid of high places.

I have always been amazed at how relatively easy it is to go into business in the United States. Consulting is a good example. We consultants sell a completely intangible product. Our results are rarely predictable and the cost for our services is usually quite high. Other service industries are much the same, down to the TV repairman and the auto mechanic. Their services are more measurable than the consultants' and, although there are frequent outcries of indignation at the rising cost of repairs, by and large their charges are in line with the work involved.

Two economic consultants joined forces and perfected the use of an input-output matrix to determine where the raw materials (input) were used in industrial plants (output). By developing data from government census figures and other sources, and having the material programmed on a computer, they were able to prepare tabulated reports consisting of sales potential broken down by state, region, county, and using plant.

Theirs is entirely a service operation—no product is involved—yet a venture capital corporation invested $300,000 for a 15 percent equity in the business, thereby valuing the total enterprise at $2 million. The consultants have also considered preparing comprehensive reports, by industry, containing all significant data in the applicable industry. These reports would provide material from as many as thirty separate government, economic, trade, and other sources under one cover.

Other companies providing a similar service have been successful in obtaining and selling technical reports prepared by people with specialized knowledge, under a royalty arrangement. These services are reliable, the information is reasonably accurate, and the price is a fraction of the cost of doing the equivalent study with in-house market research people or economists.

Larry Walters was a gregarious person with tremendous drive. He had become vice-president of a billion-dollar company at the age of twenty-eight. He knew the plastics industry and, now in his early forties, he was ready to reach out for ownership of his own enterprise. He had two alternatives: start a company from scratch, or acquire one already in existence. He decided to develop plans for both and then determine which had the most to offer.

Walters gave the embryo company a name, Advanced Packaging Technology. Working with him, I then proceeded to put together a promotion package with reliable data drawn from Walters's years of experience in the industry. The company would manufacture and market a broad range of highly profitable plastic-based packaging materials. It was intended that the corporation would penetrate a number of segments of the industrial packaging market, beginning with clear plastic bottles.

A six-week investigation of current market conditions indicated that the bottle area offered the greatest potential for immediate entry. Our plan then envisioned moving from this base into the plastic tube market segment. The latter area offered the greatest profit potential because it is a rapidly expanding market with limited sources of supply.

The report contained figures on the total clear plastic bottle and plastic tube markets for the previous five years, and projections for the current and future years. It also contained a listing of the largest users and their estimated yearly usage. Management of the promotion group had marketing contacts with all of the major accounts and could be expected to develop a significant market position with them within two years.

It was planned that Advanced Packaging would employ the most modern techniques in the industry, in order to gain a cost advantage over the competition and provide its shareholders with a high return on invested capital. The production line would be fully integrated, with automatic conveyors and a materials handling system. The heart of the production line was a third-generation extruder and blow molding machine that offered many advantages over competitors' equipment.

The promotion package contained a three-phase approach that indicated progressive movement into new fields such as egg cartons, metal tubes, aluminum aerosols, aerosol valves, and laminated tubes. Each phase was thoroughly documented with marketing, manufacturing, research and development, and financial data. It demonstrated to the prospective investor that Walters had technical knowledge of the industry and markets; the management team was highly qualified; the company was entering a growth industry with continued new product applications; there had been thorough planning of each phase of expected growth; excellent return on investment was anticipated; the latest, most efficient equipment was scheduled for use in production; there was a solid expectancy of the ability of the sales personnel to acquire key accounts and gain a significant market share in a reasonable period of time.

Concurrently with the development of the plan to start his own business, Walters also studied the alternative option of obtaining a going business.

One of the major chemical companies was in the midst of a divestiture program and was interested in spinning off a plastics division. The company had made overall investments in this operation of $25 million. The business boasted an impressive sales growth but had not become profitable at the corporate level until the previous year, when sales reached $14 million. The purchase price was $9 million. Financial arrangements were negotiable because part of the purchase price would be in the form of interest-bearing promissory notes, and current inventory would be paid on a deferred payment basis

It was anticipated that the money would be raised from private investors and financial institutions.

The division made a high-density polyethylene bottle in three manufacturing plants, located on the East Coast and in the Midwest. The plants were efficient and contained specially designed competitive equipment.

Larry Walters, his management team, and I made extensive field trips to the three plants and believed that, through greater efficiency and cost reduction, savings in excess of $300,000 could be realized.

Walters now had sufficient facts upon which to make a

management decision. Each alternative had certain advantages and disadvantages that became evident as he reviewed them in more detail.

The first alternative—starting his own business—involved the following:

- Greater risk in obtaining customers and achieving a satisfactory share of the market.
- More difficulty in obtaining financing.
- Surrender of a larger share of equity to investors.
- The necessity to sell a concept as opposed to a proven track record.
- Considerable start-up cost and working capital requirements.
- The need to obtain favorable terms from suppliers based upon expectations of future business.
- More difficulty obtaining raw materials during a period of shortages without allocation.
- Higher incidence of chance that business will not succeed.
- Opportunity to select personnel without any encumbrances.
- Initial freedom from union pressure.
- No involvement in any prior company commitments, such as a pension plan or other fringe benefits.
- Freedom to select a location for the plant in the most advantageous place.
- No encumbrances resulting from past work habits, morale problems, or other personnel influences.

The second alternative—purchasing a going business—involved these factors:

- Field trips can be made to evaluate the operation as it presently exists.
- Judgments can be exercised regarding plant facilities, customers, personnel, and other items of concern.
- Financial data can be obtained to indicate the company's previous operating results.
- Physical inventories can be taken to determine the incidence of obsolescence, scrap, and slow-moving items.

- A fair market value can be established for the business, subject to negotiation.
- The parent company may accept deferred payment, which reduces the initial capital requirements.
- Lending institutions will accept company assets for collateral on all or part of the purchase price.
- Private investors will be attracted more easily.
- Negotiated union contract commitments with plant personnel may have to be taken over.
- Some customers may be lost at the time of acquisition.
- Virtually no additional costs or any unusual expenses will be incurred during a change in management.
- Immediate saving of an amount that had been a corporate charge.

Larry Walters decided to minimize his risk by moving in the direction of the second option. Although this choice required more initial capital, he felt it put him five years ahead of starting from scratch. Walters is now a successful producer of plastic products with an $18 million operation.

Many people still begin a business with an invention or an idea on how to build the better mousetrap. These men are becoming somewhat a rarity because most research work is now done in the laboratories of the giant corporations such as General Electric, Du Pont, RCA, or IBM. The fellow with a Ph.D. and family responsibilities punches in every morning and turns on his creative switch for eight hours. This method does enable industry to develop a steady stream of improvements and advanced technology. But it does not develop the loner with the "killer instinct" or tenacity of a Thomas Edison or an Alexander Graham Bell. These men, unfortunately, are almost as extinct today as the dodo.

In this period of automation, companies are constantly looking for machines that will replace people. Henry Jones invented a machine to do just that. It is a tracer boring machine. It serves one function well. A part is machined according to the dimensions and tolerances shown on the blueprints. While the part is being produced, a tape records the operations.

The machine has then been programmed to trace subsequent parts and produce them automatically. It can be used in small and medium-sized machine shops where job shop or semi-production quantities are made. The parts produced are of consistent quality and accuracy. With over twenty-two thousand machine shops in need of this type of equipment, the tracer boring machine has a huge potential market.

A prototype model was constructed to demonstrate its application. Detailed design specifications and characteristics of the invention were thoroughly documented. The machine specifications had previously been outlined in letters of patents when patent application had been made. An independent appraisal was taken of all work done to date to establish the intrinsic value of the company. This appraisal value covered blueprints and engineering, purchased material, purchased parts, patents, and patterns.

There was no exact counterpart in the machine tool industry. On a comparative basis, the closest machine cost from $12,000 to $15,000 against a planned price for this machine in the $8,000 to $10,000 range.

I prepared the prospectus required to interest the financial community in Omnitech Industries. The financial data indicated that the company would need an initial working capitalization of $200,000. Management would seek to obtain this sum by issuing stock representing 25 percent of the common stock in blocks of ten thousand shares at a cost of $5,000 per block. Another 24 percent of the stock was authorized but unissued—to be held until 1970 and then used as a means to go public with an over-the-counter stock issue.

This latter equity capital would then be used to substantially increase the sales of the company through more aggressive advertising, sales promotion, and wider territorial coverage; and to provide sufficient funds to handle the additional inventory and cash flow requirements of the business. Under this plan, the original investors would have increased their market value more than threefold in less than two years. Management would retain a 51 percent controlling interest and would not benefit directly from the public stock issue.

The plan was executed. By purchasing parts, rather than manufacturing them, the company obtained sufficient capital to assemble a number of tracer boring machines with a minimum investment in inventory and tooling. The company was organized with the general manager doubling in brass, in the dual capacities of production superintendent and purchasing agent. A small work force was employed for the plant and office.

Ten demonstration models were built. Initially the machines were sold only on the East Coast. Allowing sufficient time for start-up tooling, purchasing lead time for purchased parts, and a 90 percent learning curve to train factory personnel, 150 orders were booked with forty machines shipped during the first year. After filling the pipeline, shipments closely paralleled orders booked except for a three-month inventory "float" of raw materials, work-in-process, and finished goods.

The public stock issue did what it was intended to do—obtain more working capital. Selling and advertising budgets were substantially increased so that the company could broaden its market penetration by selling on a nationwide basis. Omnitech Industries could now employ a sales manager to carry out the expansion program.

At this time an eighteen-inch stroke tracer boring machine was introduced to capture an additional segment of the market. Also, auxiliary equipment in the form of tape-activated devices was developed for both machines. In this manner the company began to market a complete line of machine tools for use by small and medium-sized machine shops.

The inventor remained active and available to continue much of this creative developmental work. He provided most of the future planning "brains" needed to develop additional automated equipment.

Starting with plant facilities of 4,000 square feet, within six years the company had grown to a multi-complex housed in buildings with 100,000 square feet of space.

Henry George still builds excellent mousetraps. Not the kind, perhaps, that will revolutionize our lives but sound enough to find a ready market. He's a loner and likes it that way. Maybe he's become a rare and dying species in our too well organized society.

It would be nice to contemplate what tremendous things could be done for all mankind if our many learned Ph.D.'s were sprung loose to challenge the "system" for a few short and glorious years.

4
Batten Down the Hatches

Pilferage, theft, and misappropriation of company funds have rapidly become a national scandal. The public frequently hears about prominent men in industry who get caught redhanded with their hands in the till. But these are the gentlemen of industry—they have class! For every Louis Wolfson, there are countless numbers of "little people" stealing amounts that add up to millions and, in many instances, driving their companies into bankruptcy.

As a consultant, I have witnessed ingenious schemes to bilk companies out of substantial chunks of money. Often, I am retained to analyze the operations and devise a series of controls to stop the thefts. At times I have been successful in cutting losses, and at other times I have failed. Whenever the latter situation occurred, it reminded me of the old chestnut about the Russian sentry at the Upper Slobokia Iron Works.

The sentry had been informed that someone was stealing and that he had to stop it or suffer the consequences of being banished to Siberia. The next day a worker came to the gate pushing a wheelbarrow loaded with hay. The sentry stopped the man and jabbed his bayonet into the hay. Finding nothing in the barrow, he let the worker leave the plant. This routine went on for weeks, with the same man being checked each day by the exasperated sentry who suspected him of stealing, though nothing was found in the wheelbarrows. Finally, as the reported thefts continued, the commissar of the district ordered the sentry deported to Siberia for dereliction of duty. On that last day, as he was being dragged away to the waiting van, the sentry saw the same worker approaching the gate.

In a high-pitched cry of anguish, the sentry yelled, *"Please tell me, what have you been stealing?"*

The worker looked up and nonchalantly replied, "Wheelbarrows."

Funny and farfetched—but is it? Through theft, the Dyna-Craft Yacht Company had been losing enough lumber, materials, and hardware each year to build one hundred boats. One day the controller and I were walking near the main gate when a forklift truck rumbled by, heading for the dump heap outside the plant. The load consisted of about twenty neatly nested sinks (slightly nicked in places) and many other apparently good yacht supplies.

The controller stopped the truck operator and asked him who had authorized the disposal. The truck operator showed him a move ticket with an illegible signature. The controller then instructed him to take the load to the stockroom. While he drove off, we walked to the stockroom, arriving perhaps ten minutes later. *All the items were gone.*

We asked the stockroom attendant what had happened to the material. He said that when it came in, he had put everything back in the bins—as he normally would do upon receipt of any goods—since no one had told him to do otherwise. The apparent theft had been averted. But like the Russian sentry, what do you do in a situation like this? Fire the forklift operator who insisted he was only doing his job? Or, do you fire the stockroom attendant who swore that he also was only doing his job? Or, do you fire both men on insufficient evidence that they were working in concert?

Some of the leaks were plugged by installing a serialized move ticket system, placing an audit trail on transfers in and out of the stockroom, and tightening internal controls.

Despite these improvements, I was compelled to recommend to Dyna-Craft management that it spend $80,000 repairing the chain link fence around the facility and installing spotlights at stratetgic points. A private detective agency was hired to provide twenty-four-hour surveillance and police protection. This cost another $50,000, but it was the only way to stop the drain in pilferage estimated to be running at the rate of $300,000 yearly.

Yet Dyna-Craft's loss was small potatoes compared to the plan devised to steal one million pounds of copper from United Mining and Metals. This took some doing. A truck driver for one of the major scrap dealers would drop a number of barrels off on the way to the plant. His accomplice at the company worked on the scales. When the scrap was weighed in, the accomplice would simply record the amount shown on the bill of lading. The truck driver then drove to a large Quonset hut where the scrap was commingled with other scrap. Accounting clerks meticulously posted these erroneous receipts to the raw materials ledger cards without ever spotting the shrinkage.

This went on for years, until finally the thieves had a falling out and one man blew the whistle on the scheme. At this point, United Mining and Metals did something about it. They put in a scale that recorded the weight automatically and installed tight, effective accounting controls. You can buy an awful lot of safeguards for one million pounds of scrap copper when the price of the metal reaches as high as seventy cents per pound.

Copper can be a rather expensive metal, but gold is weighed by the ounce. And Soloman and Katz were jewelers paying $180 for one troy ounce, or $2,370 a pound. Now that's the kind of stuff worth stealing. Easy to take—and easier yet to dispose of.

Mr. Katz, a short, wiry, aggressive man with an entire lifetime invested in his jewelry company, was scared. A fellow businessman had recently been forced into bankruptcy after a trusted employee had stolen thousands of dollars worth of precious metals and valuable pieces of jewelry. Mr. Katz needed, and desperately wanted, a tight inventory control system. And to be effective, the system had to encompass the complete sweep of the production cycle—from receipt of an order through shipment to the retailer. The system had to control metal and diamonds from the raw material stage through casting, stamping, filing, polishing, stone setting, and packaging.

Could I pit my consulting experience against the insidious schemes and industrial plotters lurking in the work force of Soloman and Katz? Only time would tell!

After days of detailed study, my analysis of the company's existing procedures led me to the following recommendations:

- *Diamond inventories*
  The system should be set up to control diamonds by lot number with the use of a computer. Periodic and unannounced spot audits should be made to check the physical diamond inventory against the computer reports. The diamond buyer should be charged with complete and total responsibility for the physical inventory. Withdrawals from stock should be made only upon written authorization and immediately prior to stone setting.

- *Metal and bullion inventory*
  The issuance and control of alloyed metal and bullion should be the sole responsibility of one of the partners. This metal should remain in a locked box in the vault until ready for use and then be controlled by pennyweight. All metal, when weighed, should be recorded in ink and handled only by members of management.

- *Work-in-process inventory*
  All work in process should be returned to the crib between operations. Only orders actually being worked on, or reasonably close to being worked on, should be out on the production floor.

Shop orders for stock should be scheduled by operation by the factory manager and controlled throughout the entire cycle on a visual production control board.

Special orders for smaller amounts should be controlled by a master control card.

Considering the high value of the material content compared to the low cost of containers, the company should purchase new standardized containers in which to hold metal and carry it from one operation to another.

- *Finished goods inventory*

Min-max points and reorder quantites should be established by management and constantly reviewed on all items. A stock replenishment order should be prepared when a minimum point is reached, over the signature of the factory manager.

The inventory records should show bin location numbers to speed search time and reduce errors.

All other inventory items—finished rings, mountings, components, watch cases, pendants—should be under the control of the factory manager. Components should be controlled by weight; all other items, when once identifiable, should be controlled by individual unit or piece.

- *General inventory control*

A clear separation should be made between physical inventories and the control records.

Orders showing discrepancies in weight or count should be set aside by the crib attendant for review by the factory manager.

All shortages or discrepancies must be recorded on a shortage and discrepancy report, initialed by the manager and constantly analyzed to pinpoint areas requiring corrective measures.

Periodic and spot audits should be made on physical inventories reconciled against the control records.

Lapping tools with high dollar value and any other similar tools should be maintained in the crib.

The recommendations were developed to control all types of inventories, and the systems proposed were both effective and relatively inexpensive to institute. It was also done in adherence to the axiom that "the cost of a control must never exceed the losses that might accrue if the control didn't exist."

But I wasn't satisfied with the mechanics of the system alone. I had to add a finishing touch to my work of art. And that was when the plot thickened, as they were given to say in the silent flicks.

The idea hit me that if I built a cage around the vault with only two long-time, trustworthy people on the inside—one to dispense material to the jewelers and the other to do the final packing after the items were completed in manufacturing—nothing could possibly go wrong. But in a typical small, family-run company, things did not always go according to plan.

The boss accepted the idea—in fact, he thought it was great—but with one qualification. "Jerry," he said, "I'll need access to the crib and so will my son-in-law who is part of management. Naturally, the factory manager would also have to be in the cage since he, too, needs to go to the vault occasionally. His finished goods record clerk must be in the cage as well." There were others with the same "logical" reasons for being inside rather than outside the crib area.

By the time the crib was built, there were eight people inside. And the situation became almost ludicrous because on hot, humid days when the old-timer bench workers stayed home in their apartments in Brooklyn and the Bronx, you could almost count more people in the "secured area" than out on the floor "pilfering."

I don't know the motto for this fiasco, but apparently the lesson to be learned is that any effective control must begin with the boss. He must not only endorse it and understand its purpose completely; he must also realize that the moment he assigns responsibility for specific portions of the control system to more than one person, the system becomes worthless.

In large plants the only satisfactory solution to the control of pilferage is to employ an experienced security chief. This individual can then organize the security function so that stealing will be held to an absolute minimum. Employees will soon become aware that the security force is continually making surveillance checks; enforcing use of departmental badges; supervising adherence to company rules and regulations; staying with visitors while they are in the plant; controlling all exits, entrances and the entire periphery of the plant; watching the movement of materials in and out of the facility; and controlling personnel under its jurisdiction.

In addition, the security chief should have authority over plant lighting, distribution of off-hour passes, security procedures related to packages leaving the plant, and other policing activities.

Larceny is another matter. It goes on all the time in industry and often is committed by persons who are least suspect. The small businessman who permits his bookkeeper to take the books home at night or on weekends to "catch up" is inviting theft. Yet this practice is very common. The company that employed a married couple as its timekeeper and bookkeeper was asking for trouble—and got it!

The scheme was really very simple. During the summer months, employees were given vacation pay in cash when they took their vacations. The timekeeper and the bookkeeper, working in collusion, prepared duplicate withdrawals spaced at different times during the summer—with one withdrawal going to the worker when it was due him and the other to themselves at an earlier or later time. Since the accounting system did not provide for cross-checking withdrawals by employee, the couple was able to steal about $7,000 from the company each year. After they had worked this ploy for about six years, I happened to be working with the outside accountants on a management audit when the fraud was uncovered, and they were finally apprehended.

One of the most ingenious methods of larceny that I can recall was accomplished in this manner.

The bookkeeper at Playtime Togs, a soft goods manufacturer, was responsible for accumulating piece tickets for work performed by each machine operator. Since there was a considerable amount of turnover and absenteeism, the bookkeeper would reconstruct a complete set of nonexistent piece tickets at home, during the evening, for a person who had not worked that week. The tickets, having been duly calculated and extended off-premises, would then be recorded the next day on the absent employee's ledger card. The following payday, the amount would be included in the payroll disbursement, and the bookkeeper would pocket the money falsely drawn for the absentee employee.

It was only by chance that the boss happened to recall that a certain employee had been absent during a previous week, yet had been "paid." By a painstaking payroll audit that reconstructed each worker's pay over a six-month period, the scheme was uncovered.

The credit manager at the Detroit store of Barton's, a large credit appliance chain, did the Playtime Togs' bookkeeper even one better. She devised a method that, over a few short years, resulted in the manipulation, and possible theft, of over $300,000 in company funds.

As Barton's customers failed to meet their obligations to pay their bills, the dunning procedure moved the accounts receivable card through the 30, 60, 90, and 120-day periods and finally to a collection agency. However, because of executive management pressure, the credit manager didn't want to show poor performance by having hundreds of un-collectible accounts go to the collection agency where the agency receives 40 to 50 percent of the amount collected. Instead, she devised a very simple scheme.

Each morning she ran a number of delinquent cards through the cash register to show fictitious payments. Then, within the same accounting period, she ran an offsetting entry on the cards to show a "late charge." When her scheme was finally uncovered by chance (which is usually the way it happens), the company had a whopping write-off for that year.

But the president of Barton's was about to compound the fraud. After the credit manager had been fired, she was later hired by a nearby collection agency. The president of Barton wanted to turn the company accounts over to that particular agency to see if it could make the collections. That's when a management consultant is worth his weight in gold. I intervened to stop this incredible blunder. Instead, the receivable cards were turned over to the best collection agency in that area which succeeded in recovering some of the money.

Private detective agencies can be employed to find a culprit through undercover means. The idea works occasionally, but it's also playing Russian roulette with people's lives. Therefore, hiring such an agency should be done with the utmost care and discretion.

One of my clients tried this approach when he appeared to be losing carpeting in his carpet-to-vinyl production plant. The shortages could have been legitimate, but coincidentally the president had been approached by a leading detective agency with the proposal to place an undercover security agent in the department. He agreed to try this means of "snaring the hare."

I inadvertently became involved in the plot because, while this undercover work was going on, I had been engaged to install improved administrative and operating methods in the department.

One of my recommendations was to assign specific responsibility to a few key men in critical manufacturing areas. A young fellow in the finishing department seemed to possess all the qualifications needed to handle the cutting and packaging stage in the cycle. Harry Turner was strong, alert, and intelligent, and appeared well above the average type to be found in this group.

When I recommended that Turner be given the new

responsibility, the president seemed to shy away from the suggestion without a plausible explanation. Furthermore, he said, "Turner will be going back to college in the fall, so he would only be a lead man for a few months."

"Fine," I replied, "but in the meantime he can get the operation running smoothly and also train a replacement. There's plenty of time to do both, and with his college training, he can easily handle it."

Well, the good common sense of my statement had backed poor Frank, the president, up against the wall. He had no alternative but to say, "Jerry, we can't do it because he's a security agent, and only the division head is aware that this fellow is here for that purpose."

Harry Turner worked in the department about eight weeks. He watched and followed suspects without arousing undue suspicion. He gained the confidence of other workers in casual conversation. He even followed a fellow in his car one evening when he thought the worker had taken some carpeting. Still, nothing came of it. No specific act had been uncovered.

Then, a strange thing happened. His daily reports started to describe what was going on in the department.

"The men don't respect the foreman."

"Morale is poor."

"One of the girls is running around with someone even though she is married."

"The people are taking long breaks."

"The department is sloppy."

All of it was petty gossip, typical of a small, rural community. I received copies of the reports and I soon became irritated with the nonsensical contents. They had nothing to do with his assignment and were, for the most part, a hodgepodge of innuendos. It was absolutely ridiculous to pay someone for this third-rate bunk.

I discussed the situation with the president and he agreed with my conclusion. The contract with the security agent was terminated. That type of approach is not only worthless, but downright dangerous. So a word of caution: Private detective agencies should be used with the utmost care, and the highest order of integrity in the performance of their duties should be expected from them.

The year-end physical inventory indicated that the carpeting losses were only normal shrinkage due to improper cutting, wastage, poor inventory control procedure, and bad housekeeping.

Some companies use lie detector tests when hiring all new employees. I have seen this practice badly misused. Again, the yellow caution light is blinking. Some excellent people were lost to a company because the tests recorded negative emotional reactions caused, more often than not, by the test experience itself rather than by some innate failing of the individuals.

In one case, the testing agency had a tendency to subjectively evaluate people, later using the test to "validate" its preliminary conclusions obtained during the initial interview. I found many of these test results highly suspect. Why not, I thought, go back to the ancient test of placing a heated knife on the person's tongue to see if it were parched or not? Would it really be any more reliable an indicator of a person's honesty?

Although pilferage and theft must be controlled, security agents, lie detector tests, and other such means of combatting crime should be used prudently. They are just as apt to create other problems as to solve the initial ones. Often the honest person becomes suspect while the guilty escape with apparent ease. The situation is somewhat analogous to the often-repeated statement that the screening of visitors by guards stops the innocent visitor, but never the well-prepared intruder, for he has done his homework well and knows precisely how to slip into the plant or department to which he seeks entry.

5
A Thousand and One Nights of Good Salesmanship

In the Arabian Nights tales, the main story tells of the Sultan Shahrigar, who decreed that each girl he married should be killed on the morning after the wedding. The sultan had many brides and each died in this way. But when he married Scheherazade, the sultan found himself in a different ball game. She told him a fascinating story each night—and stopped the tale at the most exciting point. The old sultan became so interested that he let Scheherazade live another day to finish the story. After a thousand and one nights (of her storytelling), he fell in love with her and changed his attitude concerning the disposition of wives. That was salesmanship with the best incentive plan ever developed!

How many salesmen have this kind of perseverance? It would take a lot of farmer's daughter jokes to keep a string like that going. But perseverance is the most important trait needed to successfully sell an idea, service, or product. Few products in history have been so great that people literally came pounding on the door of the inventor. In fact, a nameless inventor actually built the better mousetrap—one far more efficient than any then in use—yet it failed to sell because of poor promotion.

Perhaps the best anecdote ever told on the subject of perseverance in selling goes something like this :

Several years ago, a nationally prominent firm ran a contest to find the best salesman in the organization. Unexpectedly, he turned out to be an obscure cornball working out in the boondocks. The company's top brass decided to play up the situation by visiting the salesman en masse and presenting him with his prize in person. So out they went to visit the superstar. When they met him, he was most unimpressive—certainly no dynamo.

A big banquet was held and after the fried chicken and peas, the company president rose and spoke a few words of greeting. Then for the highlight of the evening, he turned to his ace salesman and said, "Tell us, Homer, what's the secret of your success? Just how do you sell so much of our products? What's your fantastic sales pitch that brings in all those juicy orders?"

Homer Yates rose slowly, looked around at the mass of eager faces with a somewhat puzzled look, and then began, "I don't rightly know what the reason is—'cause all I do is sit down with the fellow I want to sell to and show him what we have in our catalog. Then after reading what it says about each item, I ask him for the order before turning the page. Naturally, I want his business real bad, so I ask again, 'May I have your order?' after completing each one of the remaining pages."

By then the executives were dumbfounded. That meant that Homer asked for the order exactly 58 times. The vice-president of sales was the first to come out of shock and he barely made it by stammering, "But Homer, what do you do if, after you have asked for the order time after time, the potential customer still hasn't placed his business with you?"

Homer glanced up and, with a twinkle in his eyes, replied, "Mr. Johnson, when that happens, I go back to the first page and start all over."

Ours is a knockdown, drag 'em out, merchandising-oriented society. We sell planned obsolescence, disposable items, and anything else that a gullible public will buy. Through strong advertising and promotion, consumers have been persuaded to go into hock on short-term loans to the tune of over $200 billion. And, the name of the game won't change. You can *sell* people anything—bottled water, fresh air, or sunshine.

The former president of the giant Ashland Oil Company, Rexford S. Blazer, knows what the consumer is like when he says, "Expand a business by backward integration." What he means is that he oversells his refineries. He books the business first and *then* concerns himself with meeting his commitments. In Blazer's words, "A ten-thousand-barrel-a-day refinery ought to have a twenty-thousand-barrel-a-day sales organization."

When he oversells, Blazer either expands his facilities after receiving the business or he acts as a broker and buys the overage from a competitor. Henry Kaiser got into the cement business in the same way—by booking orders even before he had a plant built.

Many savvy executives wish that a big new facility sitting on top of a hill could sustain itself immediately, rather than incur substantial start-up losses for the first few years. Usually, to cover fixed period expense, the only recourse is to obtain large contract business at very favorable terms to the buyer until 75 to 80 percent of the basic cost is covered, and then gradually sell profitable business until the product mix is reversed.

Promotion and merchandising are the dual prongs needed to penetrate a market successfully. The old saw, "Say anything about me, only say something!" may be trite, but people in the limelight know that it is true. To cite one example, for many years Andy Granatelli successfully promoted STP, the "revolutionary" oil additive, racking up a tremendous boost in sales through the medium of a promotion budget that amounted to 45 cents on every dollar of actual sales. When an article in a consumer guide magazine indicated that STP did virtually nothing for an automobile engine, the bubble burst and sales came tumbling down.

We are all familiar with the huge cost of promoting cosmetics, yet for years this segment of the beauty care industry has racked up phenomenal sales and profits. Cosmetics have been merchandised by the use of tantalizing ad inducements that appeal to female vanity and woman's desire to attract and seduce the male animal.

What, then, does it take to introduce and successfully market a new product? Let's look at this unique American skill with something that really requires a professional approach—like a yacht with a price tag of $125,000.

The Ocean Breeze Yacht Company had been experiencing deep trouble until a few short years ago. It manufactured only wooden boats. One-third of its sales were of eighteen-footers, and it lost $500 on each one.

In order to survive in the fragmented boating industry, top management decided the company would have to upgrade its product line. This meant going from wood to fiberglass construction and building longer boat lengths. Fiberglass offers relatively maintenance-free care—for about 25 percent more money. Wood has a richness about it; fiberglass is sleek and functional. Most boat owners are weekend pleasure seekers who are interested in the relaxation that the sport offers. Painting, varnishing, and scrubbing the deck on hot summer days is not their cup of tea.

So Ocean Breeze, as a division of a large corporation, plowed capital into fiberglass molds, facilities, and new tooling and skimmed past the small, low-overhead, backyard boat manufacturer who built little wooden boats at a profit. Wes Thomas, the president, designed a truly beautiful yacht and called it the Sea Crest line—to break away from the Ocean Breeze identification.

Soon a twenty-seven-foot sport fisherman emerged from the prototype shop; then a thirty-three-footer; and after a few more models, a regal forty-seven-foot yacht was introduced, which set the pace in the industry for beauty and styling. Remember, though, the fellow with the best mousetrap didn't make it: So why assume that the Sea Crest fiberglass yacht would be different? Even constantly sailing the yacht up and down Chesapeake Bay, and tooting its horn, wouldn't sell enough units to pay for its paneled walls and built-in bar. It needed to be promoted with a thoughtfully executed plan.

Realizing that this flagship yacht could provide the quality image he earnestly sought for his entire product line, Wes decided to engage a professional with marketing expertise. He and Doug Carlson, his vice-president of marketing, flew to New York and met with me.

For three solid days, away from the day-to-day operations in Baltimore, we developed our basic strategies. Each phase of the marketing plan was then covered in sufficient depth to move the program forward. Over a cup of coffee, the three of us wrote Wes's first speech, which would set the tone for the promotion of Ocean Breeze's new fiberglass masterpiece. That speech was the opening salvo—given four weeks later at a carefully arranged press party at the New York Hilton.

Promotional material was printed, and advance copies were given to editors of boating industry trade journals, boating news columnists, selected dealers, large marina operators, and others attending the preview press party. Immediately afterward, full page ads were placed in yachting magazines and business publications—supported by prepared text furnished to editors and columnists.

Moving ahead, the company actively solicited new dealers. The gasoline-station-type operator, or small marina, was dropped in favor of the multifaceted, huge marine complex. Although most of these large dealers carried competing lines, their agencies were where the big boats were sold. By setting up a separate franchise arrangement for the Sea Crest line, we were able to broaden our base without adversely affecting the Ocean Breeze wooden line.

A strong marketing effort secured a franchise in West Palm Beach, Florida, and another in Stamford, Connecticut. Long Island, adjacent to New York City, is a strong boating area, so the company lined up a new dealer in Riverhead and another in Bayside, and kept a medium-sized franchiser on the south shore of the island, in Freeport. Next, franchises were established in North Miami, Chicago, Los Angeles, and San Francisco. It took a few years for Ocean Breeze to make the transition in its marketing organization, but at least twenty-three substantial agencies were floor planning the Sea Crest line.

Following the initial press party and the preparation of promotional material, our next step was to provide the dealers with in-depth knowledge about our product line and other valuable material, to enable them to sell our boats in preference to those of the competitors. To accomplish this, we developed a two-pronged approach—one aimed at strengthening the management of the dealerships, and the other directed toward raising the level of competence of the salesmen.

First, a dealer operating manual, covering all the elements needed to operate a profitable dealership, was prepared. This "how to" manual consisted of 132 varityped pages, and forty forms, that detailed all the basic requirements to be in that business. It covered subjects such as sales planning; advertising, promotion, and public relations; educational programs; selection and training of sales personnel; organization and operations; inventory control; legal, franchise, reliability, warranty, and safety standards; financial management; floor planning; pricing; maintenance, repairs and customer service; and other related services that could bring in added revenue.

Ocean Breeze management and marketing people gave dealers a thorough indoctrination in the use of the manual. Its value soon became so evident that Ocean Breeze developed a series of ten articles, drawn from material in the manual, for publication in trade magazines. This publicity served to create an image in the industry of a well-organized, professionally-managed company, and it also brought in unsolicited prospects for additional dealerships.

With the dealers becoming more astute businessmen, we were then able to concentrate on helping them upgrade their

selling efforts. We began this development process by con-
veying the message that a yacht must be sold—and that sales
planning means systematically locating prospects, moving
them through a well-conceived program until each step in the
plan is accomplished, and then selling to a satisfied customer.

The dealer learned that he needed a forecast of expected
sales months before an actual sale in order to develop the floor
plan, meet cash flow requirements, and budget expenditures.
This forecasting procedure involved the use of data, obtained
at the midsummer sales meeting, on last year's sales and sales
trend, general business and economic conditions, the state of
the money market, and local conditions.

After the sales meeting, a refined sales forecast included
more current information on purchases at the sales meeting,
Ocean Breeze's new boat line, the company's advertising
support, and other significant factors.

Once the dealers had mastered the technique of sales
forecasting, they were then ready to absorb the approach to
sales planning. It was stressed that developing a selling plan
should take a major portion of a person's time and effort. If
the planning is done thoroughly, the actual sale is merely a by-
product of this work. We emphasized that there are no
shortcuts to planning—planning takes more mental energy
than simply exchanging conversation with the prospect.

The steps in the sales planning process were these:

1. Determine who will sell boats in your dealership.
2. Establish sales quotas for each salesman, broken down by
   month to coincide with the sales forecast.
3. Analyze all selling expenses and prorate costs to the
   various markets or to the type of sales to be made, as a
   percentage that equals the total sales forecast.
4. Prepare detailed plans for boat shows, demonstration
   rides, and other activities involving exposure to potential
   customers.
5. Develop walk-in prospects, referrals, and boat show
   prospects into customers by in-depth selling.

The final stage involved the training of sales personnel in how to sell a yacht. This portion of our development plan, labeled the Executive Sales Program (ESP), became the backbone of the entire sales campaign. Its main concentration was on selective selling aimed at obtaining upper income prospects who can buy an expensive yacht. Each step of the program had been carefully developed to insure a high percentage of sales. The basic steps in "how to develop your selling ESP" were:

1. *Preplanning.* Develop the overall program, including objectives, costs, and joint dealer-manufacturer participation.
2. *Group meetings.* Have Ocean Breeze's marketing people arrange meetings with business organizations, trade groups, and associations; show films on pleasure and sport boating; and give out company product material.
3. *Qualified prospects.* Obtain qualified prospects from group meetings and develop a specific sales plan for those individuals.
4. *Cocktail party.* Invite prospects to an informal cocktail party at the dealer's showroom to begin in-depth selling. At this point, every furture encounter with the prospect should have one purpose in mind—sell a boat.
5. *Demonstration ride.* At the cocktail party, if a sale was not made, the prospect would be offered a demonstration ride in order to draw the person into boating through active participation, thereby creating enthusiasm and leading to a possible sale.
6. *Sell boat.* After the demonstration ride, bring the prospect and wife to the closing room and present them with a gift picture of the boat—then close the sale.
7. *Follow-up.* If the sale was not made, the plan called for the dealer to meet with an Ocean Breeze marketing representative and develop a continuing follow-up on the prospect.

Within the guidelines of these steps, the dealer sales force was given training on how to close a sale. The point was made that while deals and price selling were necessary on lower priced wooden boats, they were unnecessary on longer length boats of fiberglass construction.

When the decision was made to upgrade the boat "mix," Ocean Breeze recognized that its higher priced line would involve selling to a different type of customer and the sales approach must change accordingly. Price would no longer be a major factor in the sale of a boat although it still would remain an element of the transaction. Instead, the following points were covered in advising the sales force how to sell the Sea Crest line:

- Handle the transaction in a businesslike manner, with all contract forms and other papers neatly arranged and ready for use when the prospect indicates a readiness to negotiate the sale of a boat.
- Separate yourself from the marina operation in the final negotiations so that the prospects will associate you with the product you're selling.
- Sell features, since maximum profits come from selling service, quality, styling, and performance.
- In addition to knowing the product "cold," be able to explain logically and factually the competitive advantages of the Sea Crest yacht.
- Know the price of various accessories, parts, and other cost items, as well as any trade-in allowances.
- Be able to discuss credit availability, and terms and conditions of sale.
- Use a third party (friend or relative of the prospect) to advantage at various times throughout the sale, but avoid having this person at the closing.
- Since selling a boat may require months or years of follow-up, keep accurate current records and adhere to the sales planning strategy. The two key words to remember on follow-up are *planning* and *perseverance.* You have an investment in the prospect, so stay with him.

Ocean Breeze turned the corner at the following regatta. Dealers booked 50 percent more than the preceding year. Everything had finally meshed; the public was now ready to buy the Sea Crest yacht line in substantial quantities. Ocean Breeze had a glamorous product which sold the intangibles of "air, water, and sunshine" wrapped around a luxurious, floating, joy boat. But people were not fully aware of what it could offer until the company got the message across.

When it comes to plain, good, old-fashioned merchandising, nothing quite compares with operating a retail store. This truth was learned by the old-time hawkers who prowled the streets, selling their wares by outshouting and outmaneuvering competition. Gradually, these men began to realize that location was everything in (business) life, and they set up shop in fixed locations where they could permanently display their wares. The best location would be one that would ensure a steady flow of store traffic, resulting in sufficient sales volume to make a reasonable profit—and to cover the landlord's bite.

Mid-Town Jewelers owed much of its success to following a policy of locating its stores in prime downtown shopping areas. The company had been able to maintain its growth because the race riots (in the 1960s) had frightened many old-timers in the trade out of business and into retirement in Palm Beach and Miami. This reaction of the old-timers to the threat of bodily harm not only removed competition from Mid-Town, but also enabled the company to buy the stores of the retirees for sixty cents on the dollar.

Ruben Schwartz, president of the chain, realized that this avenue for growth was limited, but he was reluctant to sink money into new store locations in urban centers. He looked at how he operated, and to whom he sold, before deciding to move into other facets of the business.

Mid-Town sold to minorities—blacks, Puerto Ricans, Jamaicans, and other Spanish-speaking people—who buy largely on impulse. It used hard-sell tactics. As a credit chain, it made most of its profits from carrying charges as well as on the stiff markup.

When the federal Truth in Lending Law was passed in 1968, the company was required to show the yearly interest charges on the sales contract form. They came to a whopping 48 percent. This can amount to a tidy sum on a $149.50 TV set or a $300 diamond ring. Yet, putting down the interest charges in black and white created absolutely no discernible ripple in sales. As a matter of fact, when the chain increased the carrying charges to 63 percent eight months later, sales actually were better than ever.

All this is not to suggest that the twenty-six-store operation could rest on its laurels and merely count each day's receipts. It had to continually promote and sell its merchandise. Mid-Town runs a complex business involving a relatively fast-moving line of thousands of diverse items. Merchandise ranges from expensive jewelry and silverware to musical instruments and clocks, ice buckets and religious plaques, and TV sets and tape recorders.

Although its business is not as prone to seasonal fluctuations as the soft goods industry, 70 to 80 percent of the volume of Mid-Town's sales occur during Christmas, Easter, June, and the fall months. When nonjewelry merchandise fails to move within six months, it is marked down 20 percent; after three more months, it is reduced again; and after one year in stock it is cut to 50 percent of cost, until disposed of. Jewelry is reduced more slowly—30 percent after one year, then 50 percent of cost after eighteen months, until it is moved off the shelves.

How does a credit chain make more money? Like any respectable bank does: it penalizes its customers with a late payment charge.

How does it gain even greater profits? By following the lead of the automobile companies in selling life insurance on the merchandise it sells—and adding property insurance as well. This amounts to a tidy sum, about 5 percent on the sales contract price; approximately half of this sum is retained by Mid-Town Jewelers after a premium check is sent to the insurance company.

To obtain additional sales, the chain resorts to the standard approach of mailers, newspaper ads, and private sales. Of these, the private sales—usually held on a Wednesday night and promoted through the chain's mailing list—bring in the most business.

Store sales personnel are continuously given point-of-purchase incentives for various promotional items. California sales are common—these are tie-ins of two items, with the larger profit item being a piggyback sale on the other; or a giveaway pen and pencil set ploy in order to sell a high ticket jewelry piece.

Thanks to all these sales efforts, the stream of customers continues to flow into the Mid-Town stores. New customers are brought in through store displays and promotion—and previous customers come in when they are in the neighborhood or stopping by to make their weekly payments. On credit accounts, payment by the week is desired because so many customers are on welfare, or are low-salaried, and it's first come, first paid. If Mid-Town were to allow monthly payments, as department stores do with their more affluent customers, the delinquency rate would skyrocket.

Yet, despite this valid reason for making the customer report in fifty-two times a year, it is only the tip of the iceberg. The less obvious but even more important reason is that the lifeblood of Mid-Town's business is the Friday night and Saturday afternoon lineup at the cashier's counter waiting to make payment. For while in line, or on the way to the front door, the hapless individual is tempted, cajoled, and almost literally pounced upon by the lurking salesmen who try to entice every customer to make additional purchases.

Ghetto kids may be shoddy and ill-fed. But thanks to two dollars down and a buck a week for life, Mid-Town Jewelry Mart brings all these goodies into the otherwise barren homes of the tenement families. (That is, of course, unless the sheriff hasn't repossessed the merchandise for failure to make payment!)

Ruben Schwartz loved each and every store in the Mid-Town chain, even the ones in Hackensack, Paterson, and Passaic, New Jersey, which were now dying but were part of the inheritance from his founding father. His pride and joy was the store in Newark, New Jersey, at Broad and Market Streets. This location was comparable to Times Square in New York City, and the store grossed over one million dollars each year. But when an extremely ugly race riot erupted in downtown Newark, with the rioters gutting the block and almost destroying his store, Ruben faced the inevitable and decided to expand into the suburbs.

Since I had worked with Ruben for many years, I was not completely surprised when he sought my advice on the matter. After an evaluation of the situation that supported the need for Mid-Town to expand in another direction, we were then presented with various options. Ruben wanted to use the credit store concept in the suburbs because of the base of expertise he possessed in this segment of the jewelry industry. But I persuaded him not to do this, because people in the suburbs would not accept usurious interest charges of 63 percent; would not make weekly payments or face the stiff late-payment charges; or go for the life and property insurance gimmicks. Without these lucrative revenue producers and hard-sell merchandising, Mid-Town could never succeed in this different environment. Accordingly, the credit store approach was discarded.

That left two other alternatives—Guild or cash stores, as they are called, or discount stores. We decided to enter the Guild store market first and, once established, continue to expand by moving into discounting.

The Sutton Guild Division was formed and new store sites were selected in three suburban shopping centers. A fourth member of the division was an acquisition in West New York, New Jersey. As these stores went on stream, it became apparent that there were many trade-offs between this Guild-type enterprise and a credit operation—the Guild provided lower markup, but more expensive merchandise to sell; good cash flow, but no additional income-producing means; lower sales volume, but no credit problems or write-offs of unpaid receivables; and higher paid personnel, but less training or turnover in employment.

Although the Guild store division soon became a viable entity, on occasion it also needed a shot in the arm. In one particular instance, a plan to sharply increase sales could have created a panic situation.

West New York had been a neighborhood Guild store for forty-three years before Mid-Town acquired it. We decided to use this loyal patronage to the advantage of both ourselves and the local customers. The plan was to mail twenty-five thousand letters to residents bordering Bergenline Avenue where the store was located, offering "to share this friendship with a gigantic Christmas 'Thank You'."

Thousands of simulated "dollar" bills in denominations of $1, $5, $10, $20, $50 and $100 were printed for this promotion. A combination of these bucks totaling $187 would be enclosed with each letter, to be used toward the purchase of merchandise sold at Sutton's. The promotion letter boldly stated, "At Sutton's this is real money—to be used as a savings on a purchase in the actual amounts shown. It's like free money."

Well, the artwork was great—the "money" almost looked like real dollar bills. The plates were made and the printer was ready to place them on the press. Once run, the bogus bucks would be stuffed automatically in the envelopes with the covering letters and mailed to the lucky homeowners.

It was snowing that evening when the phone rang in the West New York store. The printer had completed part of the run. "They're coming out fine. Would you like to see them before I finish the job?" he asked me. I was tired after a long day spent with the people at the store, and my first inclination was to say, "No, go ahead."

However, for some reason that I could not explain, I opted

to drive to East Orange, New Jersey, and view the final results of our masterpiece. Forty minutes later, I was weaving through the skid-packed second floor loft toward the flat bed press that was grinding out the promotion bucks. John Harris, the printer, proudly showed me a sample of his work. It certainly was a professional job.

I nonchalantly gazed at the bills, flipping casually from one side of them to the other—when suddenly I realized something was wrong. With a sickening sensation, I saw that Harris was using the front plate to print both sides. The front plate being used contained only the amount of the bill, while the back plate qualified our "free" offer by indicating how the various denominations could be applied toward the purchase of a minimum dollar figure.

For example, a $10 Sutton's bill could be used toward any purchase over $69.95, a $50 bill toward any purchase over $349.95, and so forth. Without that connecting link in the promotion piece—without that vital back plate—we were actually giving away free money and the customers could have demanded and received merchandise with these bogus bucks. At $187 per mailing, that came to a cool half-million dollars.

Luckily, the bills could be rerun and the promotion salvaged. We even used the "dollars" for walk-in business during the holiday rush when a sale hinged on reducing the "spread." In retrospect, I realize it was my spur-of-the-moment decision to journey in the snow-filled night that saved Sutton's from being a real-life Santa that Christmas season.

After the Guild store division was functioning, we moved into a discount operation which, we soon discovered, is a completely different business from the other segments of the industry.

In discounting, the manufacturers and the discount book promoters control your destiny. About half the items are replaced each year, which virtually renders carry-over stock obsolete because most sales are made through the catalog. The name of the game is inventory control and warehouse distribution. Merchandise must be available for the customer upon request, but not in overabundant supply.

Shelf inventory is controlled with card records that note all "ins" and "outs." This system, however, is strained severely during the Christmas period. The U-Save discount division of Ruben's network of conglomerate stores relied upon a computer to calculate gross margins by product line, and to determine month-end inventories of diamonds, stone rings, and gold jewelry. Each store manager was tightly controlled with an "open to buy" amount allowed for reorders. Basic quantities were purchased centrally by the merchandise manager. Gross profit in this business can be as low as 10 percent on personal care items and small appliances—to only "keystone" (2X markup) on jewelry and diamonds. Volume must be maintained or else the average gross profit of 28 percent will rapidly sink a store below the break-even point.

Ruben was able to avoid the inventory pitfall because he had the credit chain for backup. Once each year, slow-moving items were rounded up and hauled away to credit stores. In the credit chain high markup environment, it was relatively easy to set prices at or below price levels of discount store operations and sell the items as bona fide bargains. The center-city poor would deluge these stores when this merchandise was advertised for sale.

So great was the outpouring of people for these bargains that barricades had to be built, and windows were boarded up, to protect the stores from untold destruction. Photographs were taken of the enormous crowds, to be used for promoting future "special" sale day events. It seems incredible that merchandise unneeded by the middle- to upper-income suburbanite would be fought over, at about the same price, in the downtown area.

Having closed the loop by developing three profitable divisions, Ruben could now sit back and view his empire with satisfaction. Each major segment of the marketplace was being serviced—with those who could least afford it paying the most and getting the least. It's a strange world we live in, isn't it?

It was a crisp, clear November morning at Washington International Airport. Steven Jameson, board chairman of Computer Supplies Corporation (CSC), was about to leave for company headquarters in Philadelphia. He had recently completed a two-year stint with the Small Business Administration in Washington, D.C., and was once again on the weekly shuttle run from his home in Bays Head, Maryland. I had worked with Jameson for many years, and I had arranged to meet him on this flight and finalize our unique plan to expand CSC.

From his experience at SBA, Jameson had learned that members of minority groups had difficulty getting a piece of the action in capital-intensive industries. They were relegated to the operation of small mama and papa retail outlets or service-related businesses.

CSC consisted of a nationwide network of fifteen strategically located manufacturing plants and sales service centers furnishing the computer industry with its data processing needs. The principal products supplied by CSC were tabulating cards, magnetic tape, data processing ribbons, custom and specially designed forms, and pressure sensitive labels. It was the world's second largest producer of data processing supplies.

We were no sooner airborne than Jameson summed up our plan. "We should be able to establish affiliate companies in each of the existing fifteen regions, in collaboration with minority member investment groups. The investor groups of the affiliate concerns will have controlling ownership, thereby enabling each group to operate with complete entrepreneurial autonomy, while it is also being provided with all vital supporting services by CSC.

"Jerry," he continued, "these people will need help, so the support services that we will furnish will consist of management consulting services, national marketing, personnel recruiting, personnel training, computerized central accounting, central purchasing, technical assistance, engineering and machine maintenance, and quality control services."

Jameson then added the management techniques that make or break a company by stating, "We must also provide expertise on short- and long-range planning, sales forecasting, budgetary control, cost control, cash flow analysis, data processing systems, and use of effective management controls."

Coffee and pastry had been served and we were nearing Philadelphia. This was our last discussion flight on the scheme—we were now ready to move. Jameson closed with, "Let's put together a detailed proposal on how to establish affiliate corporations, according to our plan, and let's actively begin to promote the idea."

Three weeks later the report was completed. It contained information on the computer industry, CSC's history and contributions to the data processing field, CSC products, market potential, new product applications, management experience and background, consolidated pro forma profit and loss statement, affiliate pro forma profit and loss statements, cash flow and retained earnings, and company assets.

Through contacts with people in the commerce department, SBA, various professional and business organizations, and banks, we began to obtain names of minority people interested in running their own business in an industrial environment. One such person was an ex-football player with the Atlanta Falcons, another an HEW administrator. Four black professional football players set up a syndicate to purchase three business operations in Boston, Massachusetts, and Syracuse and Rochester, New York.

Members of minority groups who are also small businessmen are eligible to receive favorable treatment through SBA set-aside contracts and the 8A program. Set-asides are a percentage of government orders that must be given to companies designated as small businesses (although not necessarily minority enterprises). The 8A program is intended to provide newly organized minority companies with up to three years of noncompetitive government business to aid them in getting established.

For example, the General Service Administration (GSA), other federal agencies, and state and local governments purchase over $15 million of tabulating cards each year. It would be possible for the minority owners under our plan to obtain substantial amounts of this business.

Many major corporations sensitive to the clamor for greater minority participation in our economy were most willing to give lucrative yearly contracts to these minority businessmen. Black salesmen were given entree to data processing departments where previous salesmen had had difficulty taking business away from entrenched competition.

Banks were eager to make commercial loans to budding entrepreneurial minority people, particularly where the financing of a new enterprise involved black bank participation as well.

Within months, all of the fifteen regional manufacturing and sales locations were actively being sought by minority interests. These interests would soon own at least 51 percent of each newly formed company, while CSC would own the remaining equity and would provide all support services for a nominal fee. At last, thanks to Steven Jameson and programs sponsored by the government, these disadvantaged people would be able to own a piece of the American free-enterprise system.

Winchester Manufacturing Company has had a remarkable growth record over the past five years. The reason for its success has been the excellent direction at the top. Corporate plans are developed thoroughly, and are carried through to completion. Each division head has considerable latitude to run the operation as he sees fit, providing the numbers come out right. Here is how one division with which I had worked closely doubled sales and increased earnings 60 percent in three short years.

The Essex Division, like most of the other divisions of Winchester, had been manufacturing oriented. Fill up machine time! Make millions and millions of pins, snaps, links, hooks and eyes, and fasteners, and someone out there in the wide, wide world of the consuming public will buy them.

That's true! You can sell trillions of these basic items because the market is enormous—but can you make a profit?

Eventually, manufacturers in Japan, West Germany, South Korea, Taiwan, and other countries saw this market too, and they moved in with cheaper labor. After all, a pin is a pin is a pin. There's not much sex appeal in pins unless you try to visualize where some may eventually be used. So Bud Taylor, vice-president and general manager of the Essex Division, decided to broaden his product line.

He acquired Sew-Rite, a company in the sewing accessories and sewing aids business with name brand identification. Sew-Rite had a window in the marketplace through chain and department stores. With this acquisition, Taylor could now merchandise Essex's small items through the acquired firm's brand name in small-quantity over-the-counter sales. The vertical fit, from Essex bulk sales through Sew-Rite packaged items and Sew-Rite unit sales, gave him a synergistic kicker of $1 + 1 = 3$. Each product line complemented the others.

No longer subject to fierce competition from the imports, Essex soon began to set new sales and profit records. The Sew-Rite merchandising flair permeated the entire divisional organization. New ideas involving package design, advertising, and selling sprang up in other product–oriented areas. Soon, similar acquisitions were made in related product lines. Nadine was purchased to move Essex into the closet accessory business. Tru-form got the division into the dress-form market segment. Acquisition of Reeves, a small knitting needle company, put Essex in the knitting and crochet market.

Manufacturing was able to expand in much the same way, by combining the requirements of each new acquisition. First, it expanded metal forming and stamping capabilities to strengthen the division's position in industrial and office product sales. Next, new plastic extruding equipment was purchased to broaden the product line to include plastic as well as metal parts.

Plastic molding facilities were then obtained to support Sew-Rite and Nadine in furthering their market penetration effort through sales of plastic trays, sewing chests, shoe boxes, and other related products.

In collaboration with Bud Taylor, I drafted a long-range product plan to lay out a program for the following five years' growth. This plan included a redefinition of the identity of the division, a restatement of product development and acquisition policies, the pinpointing of specific markets and products to aggressively build strength, and the development of strategies to accomplish these goals.

We prepared a market cone showing each business, market, market segment, and product that Essex was presently a part of, or that offered potential for future development. Each slice of the circular market cone represented a separate area of consumer need for Essex to hold, expand, or penetrate. Although sewing aids aren't much sexier than pins, the customer could identify a Sew-Rite, Nadine, Tru-form, or Reeves product by its brand name.

In a few short years, Essex had done a great job of planning its growth. Now it could rightly share the spotlight with other brand names in the Winchester "family." A brand name gives a company repeat business. The consumer comes back for more of the same thing—if he is satisfied. You cannot long survive in the competitive business jungle without constantly advertising and promoting your wares. Whatever happened to Bon Ami?

6
The Anatomy
of a Turnaround

It was close to midnight as the black Cadillac sped along the winding back road from Poughkeepsie to Denville, New York. Within minutes Roger Brill, president of the Denville Rubber Company, would engage me for a massive turnaround assignment.

"Jerry," he began, "you did a good job for me in setting up the Production Control System. It's really getting orders out on time and keeping track of every open order in the shop down to the last nut and bolt. But, quite candidly, that was only one of my problem areas. I am very concerned about the whole business; my profits are much too low. We are barely able to keep our heads above water, let alone continue to grow. Time and time again, I attend meetings like the one at the Mid-Hudson Chamber of Commerce that we just left, but all I hear is a lot of general discussion with no substance that can be applied to Denville Rubber."

His voice reflected a deep sense of urgency and concern, triggering my response, "Roger, have you ever thought about instituting a hard-hitting turnaround program?"

For a moment, Brill's strong features remained silhouetted against the window as his large frame hunched over the wheel.

Then, turning abruptly, he glanced at me and asked, "What exactly is a turnaround?"

I explained that in a turnaround, management must single-mindedly concentrate its total resources and energies on improving all company operations in a well-organized, systematic crash program aimed at obtaining immediate results. It is a no-nonsense effort that must motivate all personnel to achieve one single objective—making the company more profitable.

Unfortunately, turnarounds are associated with speculative takeovers or companies drowning in red ink. Ruthless, acquisition-bent operators are notorious for moving into a company and quickly lopping off big chunks of overhead; cannibalizing inventories; discarding temporarily depressed products or product lines; dismantling plants; and spinning off divisions and subdivisions. Some of these corporate raiders refer to their manipulations as "implementing a turnaround," but this is only a facade to conceal their unethical practices.

In certain instances, where the book value is higher than the market value of the stock, the raiders, through the sale of assets, can make it appear that they have accomplished wonders for the company. All too frequently, these short-term gains have devastating repercussions within the company and throughout the industry.

On rare occasions the wheeler-dealer succeeds, but more often the company collapses within a few years. The elephant graveyard of American industry is littered with skeletons and tusks of companies needlessly slaughtered in this way.

Conversely, a successful turnaround, implemented in time, has been of crucial importance to the perpetuation and eventual success of many concerns.

Brill's firm, the Denville Rubber Company, is nestled in a small Sleepy Hollow community and enjoys a well-justified reputation for fair and honest dealings with its employees. A marvelous employer-employee relationship had been earned and nurtured over the years through a bona fide "open door" policy. My judgment was that Brill could accomplish the needed changes with the support and participation of his own people. In that way, the benefits would be accepted and be more permanent.

When I had completed my explanation of a corporate turnaround and my appraisal of the overall situation, I then added, "Roger, let's cash in your 'good will' chips and take action!"

"Sounds like what I need, Jerry," he said. "First thing in the morning, we'll get the program on its way."

Within thirty working days, the first stages of the turn-around were an accomplished fact. The initial momentum continued to accelerate. At year's end, profits were ten times greater than those of the previous year.

Now let's look at the anatomy of a turnaround.

First, we took the profit and loss statements for the past two years and analyzed them, month by month, for indications of unusual variances in sales, cost of goods, and items of expense. Going further back, we studied these statements to detect any cyclical or industry shiftings that might not be discernible by means of monthly comparisons. Cash flow was reviewed to ascertain whether depreciation could free-up financial dollars. The debt-to-asset ratio was determined so we would be ready in the event it became necessary to borrow additional funds. From this analytical approach to the financial statements, we were then able to establish tight, but attainable, profit goals.

Next, the organization had to be realigned to provide the framework upon which to carry out the turnaround program. An organizational structure is a dynamic tool to be molded and shaped to accomplish a particular objective or mission.

In Denville's case, the company was reorganized on the basis of profit center accountability rather than the conventional method of functional specialization. This change gave certain individuals more latitude in making decisions and, conversely, made them accountable for results.

Four operating divisions were formed around markets and manufacturing capabilities: Rubber Division, Plastics

Division, Silicone Division, and Standard Products Division. Smaller product lines, such as rubber mats, bumpers, and safety guards, were folded into compatible divisions. The end result was an organization with a nucleus of management people in each division who shared common goals, rather than being at cross purposes with one another.

An extensive in-house search was made to locate managerial and technical people capable of moving into the key assignments. After carefully screening each candidate's strengths and weaknesses, we selected twenty-three individuals to spearhead the turnaround effort. We met with these division leaders in small groups in the president's office to explain the goals and solicit their support.

At one meeting I borrowed a dollar from the burly and aggressive Jon Peterson, Plastics Division foreman, and then pretended to forget to return it. After he loudly reminded me a few times that I had his dollar bill, I gave him back a penny. Holding back again, despite his outcries, I then made my point—that the dollar represented Denville Rubber's sales and the penny indicated its profits.

Later, I gave Jon a dime (which, by coincidence, turned out to be the exact ratio of our turnaround results) and said, "At least, a dime is much better than a penny. But even at that, gentlemen, the dime represents only one-tenth of the money coming into the company." Then I returned the dollar and made my final point: that even a 10 percent profit would still mean that 90 percent of every sales dollar went to suppliers, employees, and into the cost of doing business.

All the other employees in the company participated in similar meetings, with about twenty to thirty in attendance at a time. Each meeting was scheduled for about forty-five minutes and was also held in the president's office. The division heads and other key divisional people spoke for twenty to thirty minutes and then opened up the meetings for questions and discussion. These meetings were above-board and factual.

It took about four days to get the message across to all the

350-odd employees. They were given information about sales, profits, backlog of orders, customer relations, competition, and the historical perspective of the company.

Looking to the future, we told them about the products on which the company expected to concentrate its efforts; the new equipment or other capital investments which would be made; the reasons why the organization was restructured along divisional profit center lines of accountability; and how all of this would benefit them as employees of Denville Rubber. We equated wage increases and fringe benefits with the welfare of the company as a whole. Denville Rubber's success was also bread, butter, and a portable TV set on their kitchen tables.

People, people, people. Motivate them, give them recognition and a piece of the action, and you can't miss. Play games with them, be cute and ruthless, and they'll beat your brains in. After the goals had been set, the turnaround plan instituted, the organizational structure established, and the employees "charged up," these are some of the concrete changes that were made:

A sound cost accounting system, based on engineered standards instead of historical data, was installed. This meant using recognized methods-time-motion (MTM) standards to arrive at time values for each element of a job. Materials cost was obtained directly from purchase orders. Factory overhead was applied as a percentage of direct labor. (It is axiomatic in industry that the requisite for controlling costs is a well-defined cost accounting system. Since costs are used to determine selling price and profit margin, it goes without saying that the system is literally the cornerstone of a company's eventual success or failure.)

Tight budgets were developed to control divisional expenditures. These budgets covered payroll, selling and administrative expenses, purchasing, and transportation. Each division controller developed the budgets for his section, subject to executive review and approval.

Financial reports were prepared to provide division heads

and executive management with "hard" information upon which to take action. This included comparative data on actual sales against plan; profitability by customer and product; actual expenses against budget; analyses of purchased parts and materials cost; capital expenditures against budget; and bottom line division profits and return on investment. In the financial reporting hierarchy, the corporate controller was given authority to audit and control division management on any unusual variances from plan—with final review by the president.

In a manufacturing concern, it is necessary to sell a mix of products that optimizes plant capability and capacity, while at the same time satisfying the marketplace. For this reason, the sales effort was redirected from heavy orientation on sales volume to an approach that encouraged selling a combination of products that would generate the most profit.

This change in strategy was accomplished by using the newly developed cost accounting system in conjunction with a salesman's compensation plan based on a weighted product-mix formula. Thus, a salesman received maximum compensation by selling more of the higher profit items while maintaining a proper balance that would enable full utilization of plant facilities. Small accounts were phased out or dropped. Any account with actual or potential sales of over $10,000 was designated as a key account. These customers were analyzed in terms of previous sales, products purchased, and future growth potential.

This analysis involved the determination of such factors as: Who is the key purchasing decision maker (head of procurement, buyer, engineer, or other)? What manufacturing, engineering, technical or other support is needed to aid in the sale? What unique features do Denville Rubber's products offer that give them a competitive advantage? What frequency of sales calls is required? What are the competitive conditions, pricing policy, and delivery demands that must be met in order to sell Denville products?

A program to upgrade and strengthen the product line was initiated for the purpose of capturing a greater share of the market. More exotic extruded shapes, special compounds, and the matching of colors were introduced and brought substantially higher profit margins. These new product ideas included plastic highway strips, color coordination for appliance and other end-user products, special seal-tight gaskets for windows, and floor mats with company or personalized designs and coloration.

A zero defects program placed quality at the operator level—not at the inspector's bench. This resulted in a sharp reduction in rejects, rework, and scrap.

The sales mix (which is different from the product mix) was shifted from highly competitive products—such as long-run small-gauge vinyl extrusions or cut-to-size rubber gasketing material, where price was the determinant for getting the order—to proprietary items or engineered products where the company could build in specialized skills, such as windshield wiper blades, components for the electronics industry, or specially fabricated extrusions for control panels.

Research and development projects were initiated by Brad Harmon, vice-president of Rubber Division sales. Consolidating these responsibilities under the sales division head meant better planning, coordination, and setting up of priorities for items having the greatest impact on the marketplace. Sales efforts in the heavily industrialized areas of New York, New Jersey, Pennsylvania, and the Ohio complex were strengthened to substantially increase market penetration.

Certain long-term, major accounts were found to be unprofitable. These were renegotiated upward to recover costs and obtain a reasonable profit. Previously, it was regarded as acceptable to take large orders at low or nonexistent profit margins in order to absorb a portion of overhead. Although there are certain conditions in industry when this approach is valid, such as when starting up a new plant, in Denville

Rubber's case this reasoning did not apply. Denville was an ongoing business where orders of this type drastically cut into profits.

Therefore, a policy was established that large volume orders would no longer be accepted merely to absorb overhead. Again, the improved cost system demonstrated its value by enabling the company to estimate jobs more precisely and to become selective in customers and products.

Within each division, those persons responsible for purchasing were given the assignment of controlling raw materials and lowering inventory investment. To reduce costs, many blanket orders were negotiated on a large-volume repetitive items, such as office, maintenance, and hardware supplies. Specifications for compounds were reviewed and many compounds were eliminated, combined, or downgraded. Wherever purchases could be consolidated between divisions to gain price or other advantages, this was done.

The Plastics Division manufacturing facility was mechanized to increase productivity. Conveyors were installed to move material from the storage area to the miter table and press. Operations such as notching, kickpress, four-ton press, and hot blade were done in tandem.

A training program was initiated to provide competent personnel for second and third shift operations. Long-run, less complicated extrusions with basic compounds and wider dimensional tolerances were scheduled for the third shift.

Since turnover was a problem, and many operators on the second and third shifts were moonlighting, it was necessary to bolster the calibre of personnel. Until the work force could be stabilized, those with manufacturing experience were transferred from staff and service departments to key machine operator slots until new men could be trained to produce a quality product.

Lead men were placed on the second and third shifts to supervise personnel, feed work to the production floor, perform secondary machining chores, and set up and repair equipment.

Virgin raw materials and reground materials were moved to bins more easily accessible to the blenders. A new blender was purchased to provide a major portion of the plastics compound at a net savings of over four cents per pound. Daily production records were prepared to analyze excessive downtime, locate causes, and take corrective action. Air space was used to store raw materials and finished goods. Conveyors were purchased to facilitate the movement of subassemblies and finished parts in the finishing department.

The Rubber and Silicone Divisions were fully automated to provide continuous, straight-line, work-in-process flow. Less experienced employees were used in place of skilled personnel on routine, less critical, support jobs in estimating, inspection, and production control. To reduce direct labor costs, a grade B intermediate job position was established for less experienced operators in finishing.

Manpower budgets were prepared based on the sales forecast reflecting manning requirements for each operating department at various incremental levels of production. A capital equipment budget was established to set priorities for new or replacement equipment.

The corporate controller, Ken Keating, determined the earnings per share contribution expected from each operating division head. Key personnel were given incentive bonuses based on a percentage of the profit goals established for the division. Staff and service departments were also given incentives directly related to the accomplishment of division goals.

During the turnaround program, periodic progress reports were prepared for distribution to each level of management. These reports contained a summary of each project, showing the actual results to date against plan. This information was capsulated and, in turn, passed along to all employees. As a result, morale remained at a consistently high level, with complete cooperation and participation by all the staff.

Today, Denville Rubber has twice the sales volume it enjoyed five years ago, and profit margins are holding close to established goals. Roger Brill learned about executing a turnaround from firsthand experience. Since this tailor-made program worked for Denville, we may question whether it has similar application to other companies as well.

Although each turnaround situation is different—in much the same manner that every company has its unique characteristics—the basic approach is the same. Goals must be identified and established; organizational components realigned and key individuals selected; all employees brought into the program; and specific projects assigned, with actions to be taken and time frames to get the jobs done. In addition, there must be total support at the top, and full recognition for the "achievers."

Company size is not a constraint in executing a turnaround program. Denville Rubber was a medium-sized company. Walton Tobacco is the sixty-sixth largest corporation in the United States, yet the turnaround results in one of its major divisions were just as dramatic as Denville's.

The job at Walton didn't start out as a turnaround. I had been asked to look over the division and perform a management audit. But the company had been rushing toward diversification in the light of the cigarette-cancer scare, and the Carter Products Division had grown too rapidly as a result.

Starting with only a handful of employees and the captive cigarette foil production, Carter had grown in seven years to a $170 million business. Sales volume was holding steady, but profits were low. I recommended a turnaround program aimed at increasing profits by 150 percent over the previous year. The proposal was accepted by the general manager, Nelson Adams, and we were on our way.

Unlike Denville Rubber, Carter had a depth of management people who could be used for the turnaround effort and still keep the plant going. My investigation gave me an opportunity to spot the type of specialized personnel needed for a hard-hitting program. I picked about fifteen "chargers" in line and staff positions to work with me as a well-coordinated task force.

Before undertaking the specific turnaround projects, I held a number of meetings with Nelson Adams and his executive staff to prepare short- and long-range plans. Adams was a cautious, conservative, low-keyed individual who preferred to deliberate for countless moments, puffing on his pipe, before reaching a decision.

Although the company needed to move quickly, Adams's personality dictated that detailed planning must be an integral part of the turnaround process. Since the chief executive officer sets the tone for an organization, the pace of the program at Carter would be more exacting and methodical than the turnaround at Denville Rubber had been.

The product line at Carter could be categorized as follows:

1. Bare metals and industrial products.
2. Consumer products—gift wrap, florist foil, and related items.
3. Packaging and printed products—oleo wrap, baking products.
4. Laminated products—aluminum foil on tin, or other material.
5. New products—tobacco foilboard for protecting tobacco in warehouses, golf caps made of aluminum material, and special shapes for one-time aluminum disposable products, and other industrial uses.

A cost analysis, which I prepared with the assistance of the financial members of the turnaround team, indicated that none of the existing product categories was highly profitable. For instance, industrial products used in conversion to an end-use item were in highly competitive markets where price was a major factor. Much of the competition came from "garage" type operations which worked out of small plants, enjoyed low overhead, and were able to produce these products at a substantially lower unit cost than Carter.

In bare metals, we determined that it would be necessary to develop a market for light gauge metals, even though the continuous process casting technique used by the company restricted the number of specifications that could be produced. This conflict between marketplace needs and in-house capability is not uncommon in industry; but it is cause for concern since heavy capital investment is usually required to reconcile the discrepancy.

In consumer products, the study indicated that, with the exception of florist foil, the long-term profitability of the items produced did not justify the present plant and equipment capital investment

Packaging and printed products, such as food product wrap, appeared to offer the best short-range growth prospects. But the development of these items would have to be accelerated, since it normally took about six months from preliminary packaging design and print specifications to the time when an order was shipped.

Under close scrutiny, laminated products were found to be similar to consumer-type products in terms of profitability, because converting is a marginal operation at best.

In the new product area, tobacco barn foilboard and the aluminum golf hat appeared to be the only major items in the advanced research stage. Neither item appeared to show indications of offering a major contribution to the company's product line.

Once the detailed financial analysis was completed, it was then possible to develop specific turnaround objectives and projects to redirect the company's effort.

From a long-range standpoint, plans had to be developed to take into consideration plant capability; general economic trends; industrial and consumer characteristics; research and development projects; cost of money; methods of obtaining required funds; and manpower requirements.

Based upon this overall approach, it was agreed that, it would be necessary, within three years, to replace about 60 percent of the existing product line with more profitable items. The turnaround team began to move in this direction immediately, because of the long lead time involved in restructuring the company to provide plant capability more in consonance with market needs. As a result, in less than two years, a new plant was built to produce light gauge metals, and this new segment of the business grew at a compounded rate of 20 percent yearly.

Although the normal time frame for packaging and printed products—from preliminary research and development to test marketing—was six months, the pace of the turnaround program so accelerated this cycle time that new products in this profitable category came in well ahead of schedule. Another major policy decision resulting from the new product development program was the downgrading of the laminated product line. This latter shift in product mix aided the turnaround effort, since it removed a draining influence on company profits.

During the period of concerted movement in the turnaround, ten major programs were conceived and implemented with great success. They were:

1. *Plant capability study.* This study led to a decision to automate the reroll operation, the foil splicing operation, the punch press, and other manual and semi-mechanical operations. After the entire plant was upgraded, a facilities and capabilities brochure was prepared and distributed to customers of the Carter Products Division. This brochure contained information on equipment, plant facilities, product capability, and technical support, for use in obtaining the type of business that would be most advantageous to the division.

2. *Sales reorganization.* An analysis of sales statistics revealed that only 8 percent of customer inquiries resulted in orders. From 517 inquiries received, the company obtained only forty-one orders. Also, an examination of the orders booked by salesmen indicated that 85 percent of the business was produced by only a few salesmen. To correct these conditions, and to reflect the broader change in product mix and upgrading of the product line, the sales organization was changed to a product manager structure. This new structure gave Carter greater in-depth penetration of markets—partic-

ularly those newly created—and provided tighter control of salesmen, customer inquiries, and lost business.

Salesmen had previously been paid on a straight salary basis. It is widely recognized that salesmen need to be motivated with some incentive above base wages. Therefore, a weighted compensation plan based on product profitability was developed for salesmen of industrial, laminated, and printed products. An incentive plan was used for consumer products whereby, in addition to straight salary, a progressive 2 to 5 percent commission would be paid against 80 percent of quota.

A policy was instituted to make certain that inquiries would be processed promptly, customer specification sheets would be prepared on all orders, and shipping instructions would be coded to speed shipment and provide needed customer service. To control the cost of packing, standard packing instructions were developed. These specifications were prepared in detail and became part of the salesman's manual.

3. *Customer service.* In a competitive industry such as aluminum, a customer service system that provides prompt transmission of an order from the field, reliable promised delivery dates, and adherence to delivery commitments is a necessity. We installed a data communications system with two hubs—New York and Chicago—where all orders would be received and transmitted to the plant at scheduled intervals. Order status information would flow back from the plant through these centers.

4. *Production planning and control.* To ensure on-time delivery of orders, the task force undertook to strengthen the production control function. The existing system was a mere clerical operation, consisting of a rough scheduling of orders on a weekly basis. A search was made for people with manufacturing and production control experience, and some excellent candidates were found working in the factory.

Led by Jack Benton, a twenty-year veteran in the aluminum industry, the department was restructured to combine manual and computerized systems techniques. Master scheduling, machine loading, manpower and departmental effectivity reporting, and labor and material cost controls were placed on a computer.

Orders released to the manufacturing floor were controlled, operation by operation; and the more basic scheduling methods of using visual production control boards, load racks, and instantaneous two-way transmission devices between production centers and production control were employed. This realistic combination of proven techniques enabled Benton and his people to recover quickly when unforeseen events occurred, such as machine breakdowns, excessive scrap, or high incidence of absenteeism.

5. *Materials management.* The turnaround team upgraded the entire materials management function. Raw materials were placed on a computerized materials requirements planning system (MRP). This system enabled Carter to coordinate its manufacturing needs with materials purchased from outside suppliers. As a result, it was possible to slash inventories by 30 percent and achieve proportionate savings in warehouse space, interest charges, damaged goods, and materials handling expense.

6. *Control of paper stock.* In conjunction with the work done in materials management, other team members analyzed the control of paper stock which was located in a number of warehouses—and was constantly being shifted from one warehouse to another. A considerable amount of stock had been damaged by excessive handling. This inefficient system was costly in many ways: expense of paper, loss of production time, and frequent reordering of small replacement amounts.

To overcome these deficiencies, specific primary and secondary locations were assigned to each type of stock; buffer areas were established adjacent to larger, more frequently used areas, to provide flexibility in anticipation of varying degrees of stock requirements; air space was utilized to free-up valuable floor space; aisles were made clear and stock locations properly identified; and suppliers were provided with the proper core specifications to enable materials handling to pick up and transport material without damaging the rolls.

7. *Data collection system.* A system to provide information on production status, and on labor and material costs, was installed. By integrating this data collection system with the computer, it was possible to control direct labor costs by shop order, department, and operation. In addition, through a table look-up instruction on the computer, it was possible to obtain the conversion of materials usage from yards to rolls.

8. *Material usage and scrap control.* In Carter's job-shop type production, with high-speed equipment, the labor factor was the smallest direct cost element. Labor averaged 8 percent of the cost value added to product, while material content was 55 percent. This indicated to the study team that controls had to be established to reduce scrap and optimize material usage.

Economical-run quantities were developed to avoid costly losses of materials during set-up, and procedures for handling paper stock inventory and warehousing were established. In conjunction with the development of engineered standards, standard materials usage allowances were established and a continuing program of worker-awareness was inaugurated to reduce scrap throughout the plant.

9. *Purchasing.* To effect economies in purchasing, the engineering purchasing and general purchasing departments were consolidated. Engineered items were placed on the computer, as were supply items, perishable tools, and maintenance parts. All parts were classified and coded to facilitate conversion to computerization. With this computerized system, the cost of purchasing materials and other supply items was reduced by about 10 percent.

10. *Management development.* Although the turnaround program achieved its objectives, we recognized that because Carter Products was a relatively young company, its middle and lower management personnel lacked the depth of experience of comparable individuals in other companies. To accelerate growth of a selected group of key people, it was decided to institute a management development program— one that would be tailored to each individual's needs.

The program would consist of informal meetings, special assignments, rotation of duties, outside instruction courses, selected reading material, directed guidance by immediate superior, and other specific development techniques. It was to be a small group, with no more than ten in number. The people chosen would have potential to advance at least two more levels in the organization. Each person would be screened carefully and approved for the program by executive management. Development time would vary according to the requirements and capabilities of the individual.

Management development was given top priority because these hand-picked people would become the future executives of Carter Products. They were to be developed from within the company to become broad-gauged, seasoned professionals.

In its totality, this all-encompassing turnaround program resulted in a significant upgrading of the entire company within a matter of months. Among the substantial changes that occurred were increased labor productivity, lower costs, less waste, and general improvement in morale. The attainment of these goals resulted in higher profits and a return on investment above the industry average.

There is still another type of turnaround. This occurs when the management of a company needs radical surgery—on itself. Charter Rent-A-Car was that type of company. Two housewives had founded it when they were faced with middle-age boredom. Five years later, after the business had become moderately successful, their husbands, Gene and Mario, decided to join the operation.

I had performed a few consulting jobs for Gene a number of years before, when he was the president of a soft goods company. Gene was a high (blood) pressure salesman who could move merchandise off the shelf—but he knew as much about running a car rental company as Sally the carhop.

My phone rang one Monday morning. It was Gene, and he poured out all his troubles to me.

"Jerry, I'm in this damn car rental business with my wife and next-door neighbors. We're working seven days a week, eighty hours give or take a few, and my wife and I are drawing $125 bucks apiece. If I keep this up much longer, it will be a close race to see who wins—the divorce court or the mortician. I need help!"

Quickly lighting up a cigarette, I said, "O.K., Gene, tell me what's troubling you."

Gene talked on. "I just fired our accountant because he refused to certify our year-end statement. Without that, we'll have trouble borrowing more money for new cars."

"Anything else, Gene?"

"Our sales have increased to over $450,000, but we ended up the year with a profit of exactly $304.50. Unless something is done to relieve the tension and pressure, we'll be ready for the nut house. When can you come in and give us a hand?"

I moonlighted this particular assignment for a few reasons. First, I didn't want a fee from these hardworking people. And second, the place was so hectic during the day that the best time for us to meet was at night. Although I went to the company office for a few days to learn the business, become acquainted with their operating problems, and review their financial records, most of the action of reorganizing the company took place after working hours.

I immediately established a formal organization because I intensely dislike running a business by consensus. Gene Gordon was made chief executive officer, and Mario Reardon was given the job of operations manager. Mrs. Reardon would confine her duties to the bookkeeping functions. Gene's wife would handle all incoming telephone requests for car rentals and assist in the credit activity.

We converted the stationery supply room into a private office for the boss—adequate enough for him to handle general administration, marketing, and sales. His counterpart, Mario Reardon, would "keep the wheels rolling." This sharper delineation of responsibilities prevented frequent disagreements on policy and enabled employees to obtain clearer direction and more consistent supervision.

I then made a detailed financial analysis of the entire

business to determine how to increase profits. During the appraisal, I broke the company's sales into markets or businesses and then evaluated each of these separate markets on a profitability basis. This critique required me to exercise considerable judgment in determining which costs applied to each business on an actual cost, prorated, or allocated basis.

The conclusion I drew from this penetrating review was that higher profits and greater return on investment could be obtained on truck rentals and industrial sales than on other segments of company operations.

To get the turnaround moving quickly, the company leased a truck rental depot located on a main artery close to the densely populated Newark area. Also, a plan for a concerted effort to penetrate the industrial sales and rental fields was devised.

The first step in Gene's marketing and sales strategy was to locate names of industrial concerns through listings in Moody's and Thomas Register. Then, contacts were made with sales, purchasing and traffic executives of these companies to solicit contract rental agreements at substantial discounts as compared to the major car rental companies.

This strategy produced successful results within a short time. Soon, an order came in from Lennox Tool to have ten cars available each week for its route salesmen. Austin Wire needed cars for executives traveling to various plant locations, as well as for sales personnel. A food chain with stores throughout New Jersey needed cars for its management personnel and area supervisors. Also, our contacts with industrial accounts soon led to other companies in the same industries, providing a strong and growing base of highly profitable sales.

Dealer rentals were our next target. Automobile dealers are constantly seeking to gain a competitive edge and to improve customer service. Gene visited some dealers and explained that when a customer brought his car in for repair and needed another car for the day, Charter could provide that car on fifteen minutes' notice. He emphasized that with many types of cars available, all ready to roll, Charter could save the dealers money and provide them with a promotional tool. Charter made entry into this market with only a few sales calls that virtually tied up all the large automobile dealerships in that area.

The next target for expansion was the out-of-town businessman, or other guest, staying at a hotel or motel. Many of these people arrive at hotels via airport limousines or taxis and must then rely on local bus or taxi service, or on rental cars, to reach their ultimate destinations. In addition, they may want transportation for an occasional night in town or to visit a friend or relative nearby.

When our study indicated that this market offered strong potential sales, Gene made contact with various motel and hotel management branches. By offering a commission on each car rental as an incentive, he was able to bring several hotels and motels into the fold.

To provide fast service, a direct line telephone system was installed from the hotel and motel lobbies to Charter's main office. Autos could then be dispatched to the proper locations within minutes.

As the company expanded its areas of operation, it became less dependent upon the unpredictable and unprofitable yellow pages' business with which the two women had started.

Since Charter Rent-A-Car was franchised through a nationwide car rental organization, it could benefit from the services and promotion material which came with the package deal. The primary promotional benefit appeared to be the potential airport business. The franchiser ran advertisements in airline magazines comparing the lower cost of Charter's services to the better known auto rental companies.

By obtaining a parking location near the airport, using visual display signs on the major access road, dropping flyers at selected motel and industrial locations, and combining the national advertising promotion materials with local spot commercials, Charter was able to expand the airport business into a profitable market segment.

Indirect and overhead costs were slashed up and down the line. Excessive overtime was curtailed. Gasoline was purchased through competitive bidding on a contract basis. Maintenance costs were decreased drastically with better repair service. Car washing was subcontracted to an outside firm. Bank loans were secured at more favorable rates. Car usage was increased above the magic 72 percent breakeven point. More competent employees were hired at decent salaries. And Mr. and Mrs. Gene Gordon and Mr. and Mrs. Mario Reardon were put on a forty-hour work week.

In what seemed only a matter of months, the company changed completely from an undisciplined and disjointed entity to a well-managed business organization. A short time afterward, Gene sent me a postcard extolling the joys of a glorious holiday for two in Miami. The postscript on the card said, "Rented a car from one of my rivals down here. When are they going to learn to keep the ashtrays clean?"

7
Profit
Improvement
Pays Off

A profit improvement program is the younger sister of a turnaround. The company putting in little "Sis" still has enough recuperative powers left to swing around without major surgery, provided its malady is caught in time. Profit improvement aims to cut waste and inefficiency without changing the whole personality and character of the enterprise.

Northeast Paint and Varnish was a specialized manufacturer of paints, varnishes, acrylics, and pigmentation compounds. It needed to increase sales and profits beyond the relatively modest limits of recent growth and was seeking a practical means of accomplishing this expansion. Capital was expensive; a stock offering would dilute equity; but an aggressive cost reduction program could produce the internal cash flow required.

In the past, management had tried to initiate actions of this type but had never been successful in implementing a successful program. Where one division might achieve certain improvements, another division would lag behind, exerting very little effort to streamline operations.

In the previous attempts, there were no goals of attainment or incentive for executives or other members of management.

In a nutshell, without strong leadership to push a program, all these efforts had been wasted exercises in total futility. As one spokesman for the 115-year-old Northeast Paint and Varnish Company said, "This company needs a transfusion in a hurry or it will dry up and blow away."

Now executive management had changed hands. The mantle had been given to a new team led by a dynamic president, Vincent Clark, and he wanted results.

Called in by Clark, I listened as he outlined his program to the management people. He told them exactly what was to be expected of them. Vincent Clark put it on the line when he stated, "The pace will be hard, and some of you may fall by the wayside—but if you're going to play first string, that's the chance you must take." Then, in his Yankee twang, Clark ended the session with his favorite expression, "Gentlemen, we must 'cut the mustard'."

Here's what was done at Northeast to save almost $2 million in excess costs:

First, I met with each division general manager and reviewed his operation from an overall viewpoint in terms of personnel, items of expense, and basic value to the company. This appraisal then became the blueprint from which specific projects were developed for the entire profit improvement program. Working closely with each division head, I established realistic goals for each project. All told, we had over sixty major projects, with about ten to fifteen on the top priority list.

Next, we had to put a handle on each project so savings wouldn't squirt away like a drop of quicksilver under the pressure of a thumb. Accordingly, we developed a project control system containing the following information: description of project, executive responsible, gross annual savings to be effected, additional annual cost (if any), net annual savings, nonrecurring expenses, fixed capital added (if any), and capital reduced.

The project control system also included a starting date; an estimated completion date for each project; and, wherever possible, other potential benefits to be achieved.

Each project was to be controlled in four time periods showing progress in savings as a percentage of goal and dollar amount. Project data could be readily made available for analytical purposes and control by sorting into year, division, profit center, and project number.

To illustrate the impact in savings and other benefits that were derived from this profit improvement program, let's look at a few typical examples of projects that were fully implemented.

Corporate purchasing had remained organized along functional lines although the company had recently divisionalized. Northeast was heavily staffed at headquarters, but no longer needed to be. As part of the profit improvement program, people from purchasing visited plant locations, set up local buying groups, and developed buyers' guides containing vendor information on items that could be ordered locally, such as plant maintenance parts and basic operating supplies. The home office was then left with overall corporate procurement of raw materials, large volume (consolidated) items, companywide forms, and stationery supplies.

Paul Knight, the director of procurement, then restructured the headquarters department so that all remaining clerical people were placed in a centralized unit under tighter supervision. Automatic data processing equipment was installed to process purchase orders and other basic purchasing documents. Work measurement standards were established for these clerical operations. On the basis of these improvements, departmental costs were reduced by $85,000 yearly.

A year before, Northeast had acquired Forbes Paint, a company using Northeast's by-products for its own processing needs. Mainly to be near its source of supply, Forbes had located its plant near the Falls River, Detroit, facility of Northeast. The two plants had counterpart administrative and related departments: personnel, purchasing, stores, receiving, shipping, accounting, office management, and data processing.

Working closely with Ed Pettit, plant controller of Northeast, a functional analysis was made of these groups which indicated that most of the departments and their functions could be combined. Within a few months, the duplicate departments were merged, resulting in a reduction of over $250,000 in payroll expense, computer costs, and overhead.

Inventory control proved to be the biggest bonanza of all! We had targeted savings of $400,000 in inventory reductions for the program and exceeded our goal by a substantial amount.

A computerized system was designed to control different types of inventory. A small number of items invariably represents a disproportionate amount of dollars in inventory. These high ticket items were placed on tight unit control. Basic items with average turnover were programmed on the computer to be controlled by using a twelve-month moving average. Slow-moving "c" items were either dropped from the line or only produced on a special production run basis.

However, the real savings in inventory management came from production efficiency, rather than cutting down on excess material already on the shelf.

Control the manufacturing cycle and you control the resultant by-product called "inventory."

In this instance, we stole a chapter from the annals of the famous gambling casino at Monte Carlo, in the principality of Monaco.

Many methods are employed by tourists and professional gamblers alike to "beat the house" at Monte Carlo. The system that has proven to be a sometime winner is based upon the theory of probability. At the roulette table, an astute player recording every spin of the wheel can gamble that, on a random basis, certain numbers or colors are probably due to come up. And more frequently than not, this assumption proves to be correct.

Naturally, the odds are much better when you can do the

figuring on a computer. We decided to apply the mathematical technique known as the theory of probability to production planning and scheduling, using an IBM 360 model 40 computer. This required programming the computer to digest the shipping pattern for the preceding three years, and then projecting from these data a random distribution of shipments for the coming year.

Good old IBM No. 360/40 then was able to tell us how these projected shipments would influence production schedules and inventories. It was telling us, in effect, what combinations of paints to produce and when to produce them. Thus, we were able to effect substantial reductions in the inventory levels customarily maintained at each plant location throughout the country.

Cutting through administrative red tape can make a company function more smoothly because it eliminates unnecessary buck-passing and prolonged decision making. Wasted motion is expensive in time and personnel. Northeast Paint and Varnish has grown at a 20 percent compound rate since the profit improvement program was instituted. The drain on the company's resources was halted and, as a result, it then had sufficient cash flow and surplus earnings to plow back into plant improvements and acquisitions.

Friendly Bargain Stores was quite different from Northeast Paint and Varnish. Northeast was "main line," from its Penn Center, Philadelphia, address to its laboratory in Bryn Mawr (in a once proud mansion sold to the company because of its huge after-World-War-II tax burden), whereas Friendly did best in the crowded center cities of Philadelphia, Pennsylvania, and New Brunswick, Camden, and Trenton in New Jersey.

Northeast had class, dignity, and pride. Friendly was loud, arrogant, and crude. Friendly dealt with the poor, while Northeast sold its products to the large manufacturing companies through executive selling and contract negotiated prices. Northeast did have one black employee in the home office—Freddie, the previous president's personal valet. By greeting visitors in the reception area just off the elevator lobby on the fourteenth floor, Freddie saved the company from having to answer embarrassing questions raised by civil liberties groups. His mannerisms were a far cry from those of the black customers buying merchandise at Friendly on credit.

Friendly's customers smiled happily when they made their purchases, but lost those smiles when a better educated neighbor broke down the contract terms and showed how Friendly's carrying charges and markup cost almost double the amount that a store such as Strawbridge and Clothier or Wanamaker's would charge on a cash basis.

Friendly Bargain Stores also needed a profit improvement program—maybe not for the same reasons as Northeast or even the same type—but because they were alike in one respect: profits were insufficient to satisfy the ownership.

Nathan Lehman, the president of Friendly, had worked in the chain ever since coming out of the service as a Second Lieutenant in the Air Force. His uncle had started with one store on Walnut Street in Philadelphia, and over the years he had added five more stores. When his uncle retired to Florida, Nathan was in charge of these six stores, located in deteriorating urban centers and selling to a clientele that became more transient and shoddy with each passing day.

Nathan had intimate knowledge of every detail in each store—from the amount of dust allowed to collect on the Easter flowers in the window display to the size and shape of the pencils used by the clerks in the office. His method of operation was suddenly to make a spot check of a store without giving advance notice, jot down on three-by-five index cards all the trivial things that were wrong, and then use these "facts" to chew out the manager. If a customer walked into the store during the tirade, at Nathan's insistence the discussion would halt while the manager waited on the prospect.

Needless to say, there was a 50 percent turnover in

managers each year. Except for administrative promotions, only one manager had lasted more than three years. Planning was unheard of, and "budgetary control" could have been words in a foreign language. Friendly Bargain Stores had solid financial resources but virtually no profits.

After looking the situation over, I said to Nathan, "Let's toss those three-by-five cards of yours away because they're ruining your perspective. You can't get into all this detail and still expect to plan the company's growth."

First, we sat down and defined the scope and thrust of his executive responsibilities. Once this was determined, the next step was to define each store as a profit center with tight budgets covering all controllable items. Store managers would no longer be on straight incentive (which accounted for the high percentage of managerial dropouts during the slow months after Christmas), but instead would be given livable base salaries plus an override on store sales. The base salaries were determined by the size of the stores, which were classified as A, B, and C stores. Managers could expect to be promoted from a C store to a B store, and from B to A, on performance and results.

Job specifications were developed for the position of store manager in order to recruit better qualified people. These specifications were then reviewed with a number of Philadelphia-based employment agencies. They took over the job of screening applicants and selecting capable people. Within six months, each store had a manager with sufficient experience and training to administer the operation.

We decided to set two goals for the profit improvement program: 12 percent gross profit, and 20 percent return on capital investment.

The key ingredient in our strategy was to establish varying degrees of response in direct proportion to a store's need. If his profit improvement was on target, the manager would receive minimal supervision. But home office involvement would increase by degrees, as a store fell farther and farther below plan.

To enable us to move quickly when a store was in trouble, we had carefully developed contingency programs at-the-ready. All materials, personnel, and other support elements were held in reserve for these eventualities.

Each store was made a profit center. When the monthly and quarterly profit center P & L figures spelled trouble, we were prepared to take immediate action. Here's how the program worked:

Any store below plan by 5 to 10 percent was placed on the following program:

- The store manager and salesmen were required to run a closed account telephone campaign, with a free gift offer. Since the people contacted had previously purchased merchandise at Friendly, they represented excellent prospects for additional business.
- Impulse times furnished by headquarters, at cost, were to be placed in the store's lobby. The corporate merchandise manager would purchase and stock a supply of novelty goods, costume jewelry, cuff link sets, and other low priced traffic "stoppers" for this purpose.
- The store manager was required to take a traffic count of the store traffic each day and analyze the data by day and time. With this information, we were able to regulate hours and numbers of store personnel so as to provide maximum store coverage for the least amount of payroll expense.
- A formal system was established to review and constructively evaluate all sales made by each salesman. This clear involvement of the store manager in the salesmen's practices uncovered many areas for improving the selling effort.
- Headquarters provided promotional mailing literature for handouts in the outer lobby street area, to attract passersby and encourage additional store traffic.
- To encourage greater sales volume, realistic sales quotas were established for each salesman.

- During this period of concerted effort, stock clerks and cashiers were expected to "double in brass" by selling merchandise, in addition to handling their normal chores. This involved their being on the floor during lunch breaks, if there was a heavy overflow of traffic, and also during peak selling hours.
- Headquarters provided special lighting or moving objects in the window to attract attention. These units were rotated to different stores so that they were constantly in use throughout the chain.
- Records and other high traffic items were placed in the rear of the store. This method of merchandising provided the store with an opportunity to encourage the customer, either through display or by aggressive salesmanship, to purchase additional goods.
- Additional store traffic was obtained by giving "flyer" handouts at nearby bus stops.
- Early morning and evening business was encouraged by offering free coffee and doughnuts.

Stores off 10 to 25 percent were expected to follow a much tougher profit improvement program, which consisted of:

- A "clearance theme" promotion that indicated substantial reductions in price.
- A harder-hitting crash campaign of in-store selling.
- The use of stronger sales personnel, temporarily reassigned from other store locations, to increase store volume and profits.
- Offers of bigger premiums and "point of purchase" incentives to sales personnel as a reward for additional sales volume.
- Heavy telephone contacts with active accounts, to encourage people to buy more merchandise.
- Assistance of headquarters' personnel in running special night sales with offers of unusual buying opportunities.
- More liberalized credit terms in order to obtain added sales volume.

When a store missed plan by 25 percent or more, no holds were barred in the effort to shape it up quickly. These do-or-die steps included:

- Drastically cutting window prices on items that could be compared in price against competition. Use of signs and stickers to highlight these reductions in price.
- A concerted newspaper campaign to bring in customers and rekindle the potential buying power in the area.
- Replacing the store manager or ineffective sales personnel if drastic action of this type seemed necessary.
- Running a big clearance sale ad that would be stronger in intensity and broader in scope than the "clearance theme" promotion employed in the second phase of this program.
- Advertising a free gift offer in newspapers, to bring in heavy store volume and convert these people to customers.
- Placing an executive either from headquarters, supervision, or another location in the store full time. This person might be placed in charge temporarily, or he might be used as a strong backup to the store manager, depending upon the size of the store and the circumstances involved. This action would usually be taken only to bolster the operation for a relatively short period of time.
- Holding a grand reopening which would include free gifts of orchids and rulers, bunting across the front of the store, spotlights, a jazz band, other forms of entertainment, and refreshments.
- Offering a free drawing on a Honda motorcycle or similar prize. This drawing would be highly publicized, with photographs and newspaper coverage of the lucky winner.
- Analyzing the store's inventory mix to determine if too much "dead" or slow-moving merchandise existed, or if the composition of the customers had changed so drastically that a complete reevaluation of the entire operation had to be made. If so, the problem was no longer one of profit improvement, but rather involved a financial decision con-

cerning the retention of the store as a viable component of the Friendly Bargain Store Chain.

With this program, Friendly had developed a nucleus of young, aggressive executives with plenty of "pizzazz." What the chain had lacked was someone who could put a handle on the situation and channel these energies into more productive pursuits. A management organization began to take shape. Area supervisors were assigned responsibility for groups of stores and were charged with training store personnel and meeting area profit goals.

The merchandise manager, with previous store experience, was promoted to executive vice-president responsible for all chain operations. Nathan Lehman was free to concentrate on expanding the business through an aggressive acquisition campaign.

Today, less than five years after the profit improvement program was initiated, there are fourteen Friendly Bargain Stores. Of these, six are in the $1 million to $5 million sales volume class, as compared to only one store before the changes were begun. Plans are on the boards to expand further, but Friendly believes in consolidating its position before continuing its growth. It bucked a trend away from the inexpensive, low end merchandise—and won. Why fight success?

What happened to the Swenson Boat Company? Up to the opening day of the New York Boat Show in January, members of the industry were asking each other this question. Rumor had it that Swenson was finished and ready for the corporate scrap heap. Instead, the show was the culmination of a concerted profit improvement program that had brought the company back to life.

Eric Swenson, the company president, and his three younger brothers were of tough Nordic stock. They had firmly resolved to salvage the floundering operation, and they let it be known that no area of the company would be regarded as sacrosanct.

What happened made boating history. Instead of stumbling under the mounting competitive strain, this rather conservative outfit came to grips with its enormous problems and solved them, turning the cost curve downward and the loss curve into a rising profit arc.

The initial stage of this change had occurred months earlier when Eric Swenson had contacted me. Within twenty-four hours I was in his home office, meeting with family members and other key management people. We spent three days in straight-from-the-shoulder planning sessions. The outcome of these meetings was a unanimous decision to tackle the problems on all fronts, simultaneously.

One of the most serious concerns was centered in the quality of the boats. In the field, where a product is finally accepted or rejected, the Swenson image was deteriorating badly. The basic quality that did exist, particularly in hull construction, was overshadowed in the owner's mind by the irksome irritation of minor breakdowns and shoddy detailing. Dealers were castigating the company about excessively long make-ready time required to correct manufacturing deficiencies.

Thorwald Swenson, executive vice-president, and Eivind Bjork, manufacturing vice-president, took to the road to determine firsthand the exact nature of the quality situation. Meeting with Swenson dealers in groups across the country, they asked for a no-holds-barred product critique.

After they finished their whirlwind tour, the two executives compiled a list of some 200 product improvements the dealers had suggested in eighteen major categories, and they established priorities based on the frequency of mention.

A profit improvement committee was set up and met for half a day every week. The committee's scope was all-encompassing. At each meeting, an agenda listed priorities and assigned responsibility for handling them. Each person on the committee was expected to execute certain cost reduction projects, as well as fulfill his regular job functions, and so lights burned late into the night as the team tackled the changes.

One direction of this effort was in parallel assaults on

styling and quality. From field data, the styling department was made aware of design problems that required functional alterations in order to reduce quality problems. All at once, the head of design, Howard Egerson, felt he really knew what customers were asking for.

Eivind Bjork revised manufacturing procedures to meet modern production standards and reach higher quality levels. His changes included issuing pull-kits with all the parts inspected before they moved to the assembly line; assigning regular crews at each work station; improving dies and molds for accurate alignment of component parts; and producing subassemblies and assemblies in precut, precision made module construction.

At the same time, the company pumped $150,000 into an improved quality control program. A new rain check testing device helped to reduce the average number of rain leaks per boat from eight to one-third, solving the dealer's sorest point.

The purchasing department staged a full-scale quest for higher quality in purchased parts, components, and materials. For instance, in response to dealer complaints about foreign hardware, the company's new specifications called for domestic hardware in Marinium or stainless steel. Although purchasing cost was slightly higher, this greater initial cost was more than offset by reduced warranty costs and improved customer relations. The search for quality also led to improved fasteners, bilge pumps, and dozens of other parts.

To build further upon the communications success of the field visits with Swenson dealers, the marketing department established a dealer advisory panel with a rotating membership that met quarterly at the home office in Milwaukee, Wisconsin. Far from being a "yes" committee, the dealer group spoke openly with Swenson managers about problems in marketing, manufacturing, engineering, and other vital company areas.

Unclogging both internal and external communications channels, in fact, was a major key in the profit improvement program. For the first time, there was a free flow of communications between customers and the company, and also within the company. Secrets were a thing of the past. Eric Swenson defined jobs and goals, and each person then knew what was required of him.

As the program moved along, overhead costs were slashed wherever possible. In a turn of events that's ironic in today's push-button economy, even the computer was tossed out—saving $175,000. The payroll, accounts receivable, and perpetual inventory operations which the computer had handled went back to manual accounting.

"Since purchased parts and components represent 55 to 60 percent of the boat's final value," Lars Schmidt, the purchasing agent, stated, "we combined our search for better quality in purchased items with a search for economies. We had to enhance quality and cut manufacturing costs at the same time. The better boat for less had to come through value analysis."

The economy drive also led the purchasing department to redesign its forms and paperwork flow, and to reorganize the parts department for efficiency and improved service.

A joint purchasing, engineering, and manufacturing department standardization program cut the number of inventory items in half. A week-long review of hardware and fasteners dropped their number from ten thousand to five thousand items. For example, one stern light was made standard throughout the line, rather than four; and two running lights became standard, rather than six.

The flurry of profit improvement program activity was telescoped into less than six months, since September was the target for the first dealer shipments of the new line. During the anxious four months between September and the January opening of the New York Boat Show, when the real test of the quality and other changes would be under close scrutiny, the questions that concerned Swenson people were: Has the program been a success? Will the dealers and the public see the improvements?

January came, and with it came plenty of competition from other boat manufacturers. But Swenson held its own and actually had one of its best sales years on record. Even more importantly, the company made a substantial profit as well.

Reverend Parsons is a towering pillar of strength for those in need of spiritual and inspirational guidance. His blue eyes sparkle with an inner glow as he preaches from behind the pulpit, exuding complete confidence in his beliefs. People throughout the world respect him for his good work and constant efforts toward the creation of a better understanding of the fellowship of man. As a truly charismatic leader, Reverend Parsons has gained the respect and adulation of tens of thousands of people—particularly the elderly in California, Oregon, Washington, Utah, Nevada, and Arizona.

He appeals to the retirees clustered in sun-kissed condominiums and tiny, air-conditioned ranch style houses, or sequestered with their favorite daughter and benign son-in-law. These aged, who meet daily, play bridge, engage in a game of golf, visit museums, or bus to San Francisco for a show, have one consuming thing in common—they must learn to live frugally on their pensions or limited cash reserves.

Reverend Parsons had established the Bible Prayer and Joint Worship Institute to reach out to these beautiful people. He offered them guidance on family matters, prayer for those in sickness and despair, and periodic inspirational messages through a quarterly magazine entitled *Let Us All Pray and Worship Together.* They, in turn, supported his institute with generous contributions and the purchase of inspirational and spiritual books, pamphlets, and other written material.

But suddenly, the gifts and purchases dropped by an alarming 30 percent. The press would refer to the condition facing the nation as "stagflation." Old people on fixed incomes, stripped of their discretionary purchasing power, were being compelled to husband their meager savings and spend only on the basic life-sustaining needs of food, clothing, and shelter.

The institute was suddenly faced with the threat of economic extinction. Costs were outstripping income. For while the elderly were reducing their support, the cost of printing the magazine had gone up 25 percent, paper had skyrocketed 42 percent, and payroll expenditures had grown by 16 percent. What to do?

Reverend Parsons met with his managing director, Martin Lundberg, and other members of his executive staff to review this traumatic shift in public support and to determine what steps could be taken to reduce costs and remain a viable entity. After much thought and discussion, the decision was made to seek outside consulting assistance, since the institute lacked expertise in the area of cost reduction. I was engaged to assist the management and provide this necessary service.

Working in concert with Martin Lundberg, a profound and sincerely dedicated individual, I soon began to move ahead on the program. First, I used position analysis forms to record in-depth interviews taken with each person in the organization to identify existing job duties. Data on these forms were then broken down by activities, tasks, and elements of work involved.

Next, significant volume counts were obtained for each activity and task. Estimated time values, based on volume and personal observation, were assigned to each activity and task. From these data, functional analyses were made to determine the most effective grouping of activities and tasks according to the work performed.

As a result of these findings, work assignments and manpower requirements were developed, and changes in functional alignments were established. Finally, we determined the new positions which should be created so that existing personnel could be assigned to them on the basis of experience, training, and job skills.

Our study resulted in a complete restructuring of the organization, so that each person had more definitive areas of responsibility and authority. This enabled the managing director to concentrate on editorial activities, policy formulation, financial planning, and marketing, while the assistant managing director, Leonard Denning, ran the day-to-day activities.

Payroll expense was pared in line with current and projected institute income, mainly through attrition and early retirement.

Peak work loads would be handled through the use of a pool of housewives and students, rather than through employment of full-time personnel.

A tight budgetary control system was inaugurated to hold down operating expenses and payroll costs. Overtime was eliminated.

Work measurement standards were employed to monitor clerical performance and maintain the proper level of personnel in each department.

During this concentrated cost reduction program, Martin and I met frequently with Reverend Parsons. At one of these discussions, his furrowed brow reflected the inner concern that troubled his conscience during this trying period. With a deep sense of sorrow, he said, "You must do what is right and necessary to maintain our solvency. For we must continue to serve the sick, aged, and needy."

The program we established made significant advances toward our objective of stabilizing expenses in line with income. Without cutting into the muscle or fibre of the organization, we were able to replace manual typing operations with machines which automatically type predetermined paragraphs or entire letters. We consolidated the purchase of maintenance and office supplies in order to reduce expenses; drastically curtailed outside services support; arranged with the local bank to handle certain audit and control functions on incoming checks and cash; changed the layout and work flow in the printing department and the bindery; and installed a batch control system in all clerical departments to control the volume of work being processed against predetermined clerical work measurement standards.

Once again, Martin and I met with Reverend Parsons, but

this time our meeting dealt with the subject of marketing and promotion. My study had shown that the institute was spending a disproportionate amount of its monies on promotions that were the lowest revenue producers.

I explained, "Income is the product of a mix of markets or promotions. Costs are a by-product of the degree to which the institute engages in a number of markets or services, each of which is directed toward a particular segment of contributors. Although there may be some overlap in these markets, each has its own unique characteristics." I then discussed these various markets. They included large contributors; those who contributed only a small sum to the upkeep of the magazine; buyers of books; those who left bequests through deferred giving; purchasers of Christmas greeting cards; those who were in need of constant spiritual and inspirational assistance; and persons in various categories who requested copies of material in Braille; taped material for prisons and the ministry; copies of a bedside library for hospital patients, and sermon material for military installations.

The assignment was now completed. Costs had been kept in check. The management group had budgets, clerical work measurement controls, and other devices needed to stabilize the institute's financial situation until the national economic picture improved. It also had revised marketing strategies that could be employed to redirect the institute's promotion effort and reach more profitable market segments.

People require spiritual and inspirational sustenance in much the same manner as the body hungers for satisfaction of its purely physical wants. It would indeed have been a pity if, for purely economic reasons, the institute had been unable to satisfy the needs of its adherents.

8
Valhalla, Shangri-La, Utopia, and the Land of Oz

What do the four mythical places in the chapter title have in common? That's right, they all represent the ultimate—the never-never land of perfection.[1] But they also typify wishful dreams never achieved in reality.

The age of the computer has arrived, with all its virtues and many flaws. Unfortunately, too many senior executives regard the computer as the cure-all that will solve their paperwork problems. Instead, a computer should be recognized as a very advanced tool with which to process unlimited combinations of data, but full cognizance should be taken of the laborious effort required to program every minute step in each application, and to build in each decision element.

Many of us have attended seminars where the manager of data processing has proudly described a sophisticated, computerized system that, upon completion, will have consumed the equivalent of thirty man-years of systems design

[1] Valhalla: The hall of immortality into which the souls of heroes slain in battle are received.

Shangri-La: A paradise on earth.

Utopia: An imaginary place enjoying perfection in government and social conditions.

Land of Oz: A mythical country where everything is peachy dandy, including a young and innocent Judy Garland.

and programming effort. Sometimes I wonder if he really means that the system will actually be going on stream thirty years hence—often this would be a more realistic timetable than the one he is touting.

At the end of the 1950s, during the prime period of unit-processing tabulating equipment, it was normal procedure for a tab supervisor to churn out a badly needed report in a matter of days. At that time, he had only to "wire the board" on an IBM 402, 403, or 407 accounting machine (printer) and a 602A or 604 calculator to get the desired results. Soon the machines would respond with 150 lines per minute of vital information on sales by customer, product, or territory; salesmen's commissions; aging of accounts receivable; incentive pay; hourly and salary payroll; finished goods inventory; budgets; or even complete general accounting.

Granted, these earlier machines lacked the horsepower of a computer to handle complex mathematical problems. They were not so adept at manipulating data, nor could they compare in speed to a computer's ability in processing a high-volume job. But for most basic, down-the-pike systems, the conventional equipment performed its chores in yeoman style. Now, in its place, we have the monster. What can we do to cope with this monster and get action from it, instead of mere promises?

Let's look at what has happened. In the fifties, a systems analyst would obtain the information he needed from one or two key people, prepare a flow chart, design a card layout (or multiple card layout), draw the report format, discuss the general makeup with the tab supervisor, and be in operation a few days later.

Today, the story is very different. Specialization has grown to such dimensions that the same system would require a procedure something like this: At the beginning, a number of meetings between many department heads and staff people would be held to decide on the "concept" and "need" of the system. A written cost justification proposal would follow.

After months of further discussion and delay, the project would finally get the go-ahead and be turned over to the manager of systems. He, in turn, would schedule the project and assign it to one of his section heads. The section head would then assume the role of inside coordinator of the project.

The job would eventually work itself down through the layers of middle management advisors and approvers to a collection of systems designers and analysts, senior programmers, programmers, and hardware support personnel. Finally, it would be completed, after passing through three generations of people responsible for developing the basic systems design, the design specification, the program interface specification, the program implementation description, the logical flow charts, the detailed flow charts, a program listing, the input/output record formats, and the report formats.

Perhaps this assessment of the present-day computer is too harsh. After all, who knows what life may be like when we are confronted with the human-like presence of a computerized "HAL," as depicted in the film *2001: A Space Odyssey.*

Flight simulators can help save lives. They are used to train inexperienced pilots, or pilots seeking to advance their skills, on the ground rather than in the air. These simulators are highly complex mechanisms that duplicate virtually everything that a plane may do under the most severe flight conditions. The simulator looks like an actual airplane cockpit, and its instruments which record the gyrations and maneuvers devised for training purposes are wired into a highly specialized computer. Any movement from ascent to landing is instantaneously computed and reported back to the "pilot." The simulator can be programmed to react to stalls, spins, flight patterns, hazardous weather conditions, and other unexpected emergencies.

A prominent aerospace company had a division that manufactured aircraft flight simulators. These critically sensitive products had as many as 15,000 individual parts, each of which at one time or another needed to be identified and controlled.

I was retained by Hilton Bixby, vice-president of the Electronics Division, to design a computerized project control system.

Bixby, a hard-nosed West Point graduate, said, "Jerry, we sell sophisticated electronic hardware, yet our division is still in the most primitive state when it comes to using electronic means for collecting information. I'd like to be able to have instantaneous real-time data upon which to base decisions." Then, as an afterthought, Bixby added, "Last week, I visited a customer who had a visual display on his desk. He was able to key-in at will and find out a great deal—including his schedule for the week. That little gadget in my office would be a terrific marketing aid when customers visit our plant. See what you can do to include it in the entire package."

It was shortly after this discussion that I stated to division management what I understood to be the objectives of the program:

• Develop a total information system that will provide management with immediate and reliable data on each project.
• Provide a system for measuring project costs against reliable estimates and standards.
• Enable the division to perform more profitably within project estimates and budgets.
• Provide for the retention of project cost data in a retrieval system for use in preparing future estimates.

Bixby and his people agreed to these goals and we were soon involved in the details of achieving them.

The first step required the establishment of a complete estimated hardware bill of materials and a software bill of materials. The data were keypunched from detailed estimate sheets prepared from previous projects.

The system was then designed to match engineering releases, after final design work and drafting, with the estimate by page and line number. At this point, the computer was programmed to compare, and replace, the item on the estimate with the actual part or assembly number.

After this step, the program compared purchase orders on outside purchases and labor expense on in-plant work for cost comparisons against estimate.

Purchasing data were key-entered from purchase orders and eventually closed out through an offsetting entry when materials were received.

To speed up the entry of data into the real-time computerized system, direct labor reporting was done through the installation of seven data collection units. Because the product was heavily engineered, direct labor control required that engineering and drafting personnel be regarded as direct cost, as well as shop personnel.

Material usage was obtained through key-entry into the computer of each stock withdrawal transaction.

As information flowed through the system, actual costs were compared against estimates, and through an explosion routine the entire 15,000-part bill of materials was updated from the lowest subassembly to the unit being produced.

Hilton Bixby and the heads of the finance, manufacturing, and engineering departments could key-in and obtain instantaneous data on four visual display screens with an on-line remote printer to retain selected data. The visual displays had been programmed to show four basic types of formatted information. These formats covered project costs, departmental costs, direct labor costs, and materials costs.

In addition to this instantaneous overview control, the computer provided many valuable secondary reports to management. These included data on assembly and component parts estimates against actuals, engineering changes, machine loading, production requirements, fabrication and assembly schedules, drafting standards against actuals, shop standards against actuals, purchasing dollar commitments and purchasing lead times, budget and cost evaluation, shipping commitments, complete bills of materials, engineering design data, engineering release and parts lists, manufacturing effectiveness, and drafting and engineering effectiveness.

The Electronics Division now had a handle on project costs—and the capacity to expand into other computer applications. Soon Bixby would be pushing buttons on the visual display unit in the presence of his customers, in order to encourage additional business. Behold, the electronic wizard had become a member of the sales team!

Now let's look at a totally different situation to illustrate how computers can affect businesses in some unusual ways. Here's the entire story as best it can be reconstructed.

During the spring and early summer months, farmers from the agricultural belt extending across the southwestern region of New Jersey and the Atlantic seaboard area adjacent to the Camden-Philadelphia complex would drive their beat-up trucks to a sprawling fertilizer plant. There they would wait, for seemingly interminable hours, in the hot sun for their turn to purchase the proper mixture of nitrogen-rich fertilizer. With the help of the fertilizer, the land would produce strawberries, asparagus, green beans, and tomatoes for market.

"But why did it take so long to get the damn fertilizer?" questioned the farmers.

This plant, like most others, had the various ingredients for the fertilizer mix stored separately in wood-partitioned bins about thirty feet high. There were perhaps twenty of these bins. When a farmer requested a certain mixture of organic or inorganic chemicals, a mammoth shovel would rumble over to the proper bins, reach in, scoop up the desired quantity of material, and deposit it in a hopper. When all the ingredients were collected, the hopper attendant would release the fertilizer into takeaway sacks. Since each farmer had his own particular blend of fertilizer that seemed to work best for him, it appeared impossible to consider prepackaging the wide variety of mixtures.

The situation would have remained unsolvable except for two innovations: the development of operations research to resolve problems of this type, and the advent of the computer.

The data supplied by operations research methodology, when programmed, tested, and validated on an electronic brain, provided the answer to how the fertilizer could be prepackaged.

Here's how it was done. First, the last two years of sales, by product and day sold, were reconstructed from invoices. Then these data were summarized by product and by pounds sold each day, and were listed from the lowest to the highest individual daily volume. These figures were then used to develop histograms[2] of selling days by volume classes. Each volume class represented 10,000 pounds of material sold. The computer then determined the frequency of days in each volume class and cumulated these frequencies from the lowest to the highest class.

Now we were ready to zero in on the answer. We plotted these cumulative frequencies in the form of an ogee.[3] With this curve, we were able to develop a model of a random sales pattern and use it to generate future sales projections. We could then establish a cause-and-effect relationship of sales to production and inventories.

Our findings showed that the fertilizer could be prepackaged—in amounts based on the "standard" sales pattern—and not only would the proper inventory be available for the farmers, but the inventory could be reduced by 500,000 pounds per month. With normal carrying charges of 20 to 30 percent for stocking finished goods inventory, the dollar savings were substantial.

Of even greater importance was the improvement achieved in manufacturing. Previously, production scheduling decisions were made on a daily basis by reviewing each day's sales, the orders received, current inventories, and immediate production needs. Now, two other factors were taken into

[2] A histogram is a graph of a frequency distribution in which equal intervals of values are marked on a horizontal axis, and the frequency corresponding to each interval is indicated by the height of a rectangle having the interval as its base.

[3] An ogee is a double curve (like the letter S) formed by the union of a concave and a convex line.

consideration. First, cumulative sales—a more sensitive indicator—were used, and second, control limits were established to measure deviations of cumulative sales. To ensure a 95 percent probability of producing the proper inventory mix, the upper and lower control limits were set at a mathematically computed standard deviation of 2 sigma.

From these data, twenty-eight-day production schedules were established with constant, uniform production. As long as the cumulative sales stayed within the 2 sigma limit band, no change was made in the production schedule. Only when the cumulative trend line went outside the control band was any action required.

Since actual demand closely followed the standard sales pattern, virtually no changes in production occurred. Where the former, unplanned method had necessitated variations in daily production from 20,000 pounds to 1,408,100 pounds, the new system maintained a rate between 540,000 pounds and 1,080 pounds. Also, the previous method had required that the plant operate five months out of twelve on a two-shift basis, while the new method required only partial second-shift operations during two months of the year.

The New Jersey farmers could not have cared less about what was needed to keep their waiting time down to a minimum. Words such as "operations research" and "computers" were just a lot of complicated mumbo jumbo that was way over their heads. But once the new system got those sacks of fertilizer loaded on their trucks within twenty minutes, they had all that additional time to spend plowing and fertilizing their land.

Westport Manufacturing is a major producer of spot-welding equipment for the appliance and automotive industries. It can produce anything from a general-purpose, in-line spot welder to a 100-foot, multi-head, specialized welder that can seam-weld refrigerator canisters at the rate of 1,000 per hour.

Located in Cleveland, Ohio, with a smaller manufacturing plant in Dayton, Ohio, Westport has grown from an engineering company to one that both engineers and manufactures the product. During its growth, it had maintained tight, centralized control with all direction coming from the people in Cleveland. Now it had to decide whether the umbilical cord could be severed and the Dayton facility could be given more on-site latitude in making decisions. What brought this to a head was an evaluation of the company's computer needs.

Westport's evolutionary development in data processing had been from unit-processing equipment to an IBM 1401; then to a 360/Model 30; and now to consideration of a fourth generation IBM 370/Model 35. Its alternative to increasing computer processing capability in Cleveland was to remain with the 360 series or upgrade laterally to a 370/Model 115 or 125 and install a minicomputer in Dayton.

Called in to make a feasibility study, I immediately took stock of the situation. The Cleveland data processing department was currently processing fourteen basic systems "loops" and had two additional systems in development with implementation targeted for the following quarter. It was also engaged in completing a number of 1401 systems conversions.

Plans had been formulated to begin programming the initial phase of a production control system that would govern production at both plants. This system would contain elements of order status reporting, scheduling, machine loading, inventory control, and cost accounting. Now the big questions were whether to centralize production control or to decentralize it, and whether to retain all operating decision making in the home office or delegate some of this authority to personnel in Dayton.

The computer industry had unparalleled growth in the 1960s and 1970s. From slightly over $1 billion in sales in 1960, the industry shot up to $12.3 billion in 1970, and sales are expected to reach $27.5 billion in 1975. There were 4,500 computers in use in 1960, with deliveries averaging 1,000 a year. The annual shipment rate grew to 7,000 in 1965, to 18,000 in 1970, and was projected to reach 46,000 units by 1975.

However, in the early 1970s there was a decided shift away from large-frame computers to medium-scale units and minicomputers. In fact, the fastest growing segment of the computer market today is in minicomputers that are utilized for monitoring and control applications. These machines are being used increasingly in manufacturing systems. The growth rate of production of these machines has been from an insignificant number in the 1960s to over 5,000 units in 1970, with expectations that it will reach an estimated 22,000 in 1975.

An analysis of the work performed in Westport's two plants indicated that they were basically self-contained entities, and that to rely on transmission of production data from Dayton to Cleveland, and back again, would be costly and time-consuming.

Spot-welding equipment is a highly engineered product. Frequently, on special-purpose machines, parts must be modified or changed in production. When such a situation occurred, it would be extremely cumbersome for Dayton to have to notify Cleveland and wait for design engineering instructions before proceeding. Usually, scheduling constraints dictated immediate resolution of the problem on the production floor—with confirming approval to follow.

When all the facts were correlated, the pieces fell into place. The need for Dayton to have on-premises computer capability in the area of production control appeared to be essential. The computer industry had moved to satisfy this need in the marketplace by developing relatively inexpensive minicomputers. A minicomputer could be purchased for $25,000 to $35,000, and the specialized software package could be obtained from the manufacturer for another $15,000 to $20,000. The entire cost to make Dayton a totally independent operating plant would be about $60,000. In comparison, it would cost about $2,500 per month—or $30,000 each year—in rental charges to upgrade the Cleveland computer facility, plus the added cost of transmission equipment.

The final numbers were in, the total system had been analyzed in-depth, and the decision was made to go the route of a minicomputer.

A company whose main business is assembling a product must have all component parts and subassemblies available when the unit is scheduled to be put together. The latest computerized technique that is used to accomplish this herculean task is material requirements planning (MRP).

State and federal laws are mandating compliance to anti-pollution standards aimed at cleaning up the air in cities. Harvey Test Products is dead-center in the middle of this force-feeding of environmental controls. Harvey makes engine and exhaust emission analyzer test equipment. These units consist of diodes, transistors, multiple lengths of wiring, sheet metal parts, cabinets, and instrumentation panels. With the exception of sheet metal parts, most of the components are purchased from outside suppliers.

Lead times are critical, with special electronic parts extending up to six-months' delivery and motors as long as one year. With states such as California, Colorado, and New Jersey passing legislation requiring service stations and diagnostic centers to have emission-testing devices, Harvey needed a computerized planning mechanism that would meet the expected rise in sales. MRP was the answer.

Working closely with the managers of manufacturing, production control, and data processing, I began to set up the MRP system. A bill of material was prepared for each assembled product, listing all component parts. This bill of material became the product structure for entry into the computer.

At the same time, we developed a master production schedule of future production requirements, specified by date and quantity. This schedule reflected management inventory policy as well as customer demand. The demand came from the order backlog, or sales forecast, or a combination of both. It was then up to Harvey's executive management to determine if there was sufficient capacity to execute the schedule. If not, the schedule had to be adjusted or added capacity made available. Failure to recognize this requirement in the planning stage could create the following problems:

* Excess work-in-process inventory.
* High expedite costs.
* Missed deliveries.
* High material-handling costs.
* Wrong priorities.

What the master production schedule did was to convert the customers' finished goods demand into a workable plan for the use of materials, manpower, and equipment. These data then became input into the inventory management function. Inventory management then established order priorities and priorities for parts and subassemblies that make up the finished product. These priorities then dictated release of orders to purchasing or manufacturing.

Normal inventory control procedures establish an order point, quantity on hand and when to replenish it, and a safety stock factor. Greater sophistication has been achieved by the use of statistical inventory control mechanisms to reduce the "cushion," while minimizing stockouts.

But MRP goes beyond either of these methods. It literally explodes the bill of material based upon procurement lead times, manufacturing time cycles, and assembly schedules—down to each component part or subassembly. Thus, every update on the computer—when material is received, produced, or assembled—is instantaneously used to generate an immediate action response. In the same manner, a change in the sales forecast, or a shift in customer demand, is promptly reflected in the computerized system. This is done by projecting a balance-on-hand figure for each component part at various points in the future.

The Harvey computerized MRP system worked, and soon

materials were flowing into the plant only when needed. Manufacturing was making sheet metal parts and assembling units with virtually no disruption caused by lack of materials, parts, or subassemblies; and inventories were substantially reduced.

Strange, I thought, this is the same principle the elder Henry Ford employed back in the 1930s. He, too, coordinated shipments from outside vendors to coincide with production schedules. But Ford did not forecast his market or employ a cost accounting system; and when he was eased out of the seat of power, his company was losing money at the rate of $1 million per day.

Although a genius at mass production methods, Henry Ford lost control of his business in other areas. But he did have a toe in the door of MRP, even though he had to work without the sophisticated data and raw power provided by today's computer. The approach was the same—don't carry excess inventory; simply plan your requirements so that when you are ready to put a product together, everything needed has arrived with split-second timing.

Graphic Sports News and Views had everything going for it. As a specialty magazine, it was riding the crest of a trend away from general publications like the defunct *Life, Look,* and *Saturday Evening Post.* It had built up a loyal, sports-minded readership in a concentrated market segment of the publishing industry.

Subscribers had embraced the magazine's punchy artwork, its action-filled photos, and the fast-moving copy which created a living image of a sporting event or provided a sharply focused insight into a sports-related personage. With stories supplied by aggressive, on-the-spot roving reporters supported by skilled, journalistic staff editors, the magazine's impact on its readers ranged from a lightning-sharp rapier thrust to the bone-crushing charge of a 220-pound fullback.

Success had truly crowned this timely magazine. Yet its outstanding growth was suddenly threatening to destroy it.

Deluged with new subscribers and renewals, its overloaded subscription department could no longer get issues out on time. When subscribers moved to new locations, processing the changes of address took months. Billing adjustments and customer service complaints were going unheeded because the system was unable to cope with the deluge of "white mail" correspondence. Just as the "back room" operations had destroyed many Wall Street brokerage firms in the late 1960s, the subscription fulfillment "back room" activities of the publishing business were taking their toll on this heady magazine.

For a yearly tab of $4.85, *Graphic Sports News and Views* had to set up an individual subscriber record, keep the record current, maintain a donor/recipient cross-index file,[4] handle all complaints and adjustments, send up to seven invoice dunnings, mail as many as a dozen renewal efforts to retain a recalcitrant subscriber, and print and distribute 128 pages of readable material every other week.

In twelve short years the publication had expanded from a three-room loft on the seedy south side of Chicago to a seven-story complex four blocks from the Loop. Its circulation had grown to almost 2 million subscribers; and each and every one expected personalized service—from Dr. Brown who moved across town and demanded that a copy be in his new waiting room without a disruptive delivery gap, to Uncle Willie who received the first issue of his Christmas gift subscription just prior to the holiday, with a handwritten, personalized Christmas card enclosed from "Your loving nephew, Timothy." At times, the magazine was almost inundated by a flood of reader mail reacting to a hard-hitting article. For example, it took six clerks three weeks to fend off three thousand irate subscribers who responded to the bigger-than-life expose of the Boston Bullets' basketball flash, Woody Grant.

---

[4] The term "donor/recipient" refers to a situation where an individual gives a gift subscription to a friend or relative.

In sheer desperation, the board of directors met and decided to upgrade the internal subscription fulfillment operation immediately by converting from the inadequate manual addressograph plate system to a computer. Philip Brach, the president, was authorized to seek outside consulting assistance because the firm lacked in-house expertise in this specialized field.

Brach, a tall, lithe, energetic individual with a deeply rooted Midwest heritage, contacted me to undertake the assignment. His only instructions were, "Mr. Fuchs, we need facts. Dissociate yourself from the mess we are in and make an objective appraisal. Give us your frank advice about what we should do, and how it can be done."

Two weeks later, I began the study at *Graphic Sports News and Views*. My approach was to gather detailed data on every facet of the subscription fulfillment operation. This involved in-depth interviews with each supervisor and key person in mail opening, mail breakdown, order markup, plate processing, gift-card preparation, file room, billing, complaints and adjustments, printing, addressing and inserting, and shipping.

Volume counts were obtained, forms and reports were collected, and each step in the flow was meticulously classified and charted. Accurate measurements were taken of significant swings in activity between various months and seasons of the publishing year. I assimilated information on donor/recipients and industrial business as well as on single subscribers. Soon, the data began to form a pattern, and the precise type and form of computerized system that would best do the job began to crystallize.

The company had 1.9 million subscribers. About 700,000 of these subscribers were recipients of gift subscriptions from 300,000 donors (each donor gave, roughly, 2½ gift subscriptions). The magazine had received over 175,000 subscriber complaints during the preceding year. In terms of paperwork volume, the orders and payments came to over 3.5

million individual documents. The seasonal variation was from a monthly low of 200,000 items to a high of 600,000.

Americans have become extremely mobile, a fact reflected in over 300,000 address changes (chadds) during the year. In addition, the publishers ran promotions to obtain new subscribers, sell sporting journals and books, reactivate past subscribers from the "morgue" file, and offer low-cost Christmas gift subscriptions.

When all the various elements at last began to blend into a composite montage, I was able to move to another phase of the project. This involved developing technical specifications containing the exact volume characteristics and data needs of *Graphic Sports News and Views*. Now we were ready to contact reliable hardware manufacturers of computer equipment and computer service bureaus, to obtain bid proposals.

In my discussions with Philip Brach and Ted Evershevski, his subscription fulfillment manager, we had decided that we would check out both options of either installing an on-premises computer facility or having the work done by a computer service bureau. We were seeking to evaluate these factors: rental and maintenance costs, or unit processing cost; one-time start-up expense; software and technical support; equipment or outside services reliability; rejection rate; and audit trails and controls. From material provided to us in the bid proposals, we were able to reach a conclusion as to the best course of action and prepare a final report for review by the board.

The substance of our report was a recommendation to install an on-premises computer, with key to tape computer entry, and a scanning device to permit direct input to magnetic tape on invoices, renewals, and other turnaround documents mailed to subscribers.

The board approved the plan and requested that I remain to spearhead the program. I was to work closely with Ted, with Hugh Frost, his plate processing supervisor, and with

Mary Bee, head of systems and procedures. Operating as a team, with myself as project coordinator, we were to get on-line with the least amount of problems, within a tight but attainable time frame, and holding to the cost estimates shown in the report.

Our first order of business was to develop a detailed schedule of installation. This required establishing the sequence and time element of each task to be accomplished. When completed, the schedule indicated that it would be necessary to execute 268 individual tasks, over an eight-month period, to achieve our objective.

Of these, the major tasks involved finalizing hardware specifications and ordering equipment; determining the location of the computer facility; coordinating activities of outside electrical, plumbing, flooring, and air-conditioning contractors; recruiting and hiring personnel for the computer facility; supervising the programming effort; purchasing peripheral equipment, forms, and supplies; converting from addressograph plates to magnetic tape; training computer and key entry operators; establishing a tape library; developing security measures and master file controls; investigating and obtaining an optical scanning machine; developing personnel policies to minimize the effect the changeover would have on company employees; determining how to handle remaining noncomputerized activities; and smoothly shifting the printing, addressing, and mailing of magazine issues, invoices, and renewals from manual methods to a computer-oriented approach.

One of the most important elements in this program was the entering of data into the computer. In 1960, key punch was the only entry method; now there are two additional methods, key to disc and key to tape. But, also since 1960, input volume in general has gone up three times, and payroll has doubled in ten years.

Accordingly, though the computer system was designed for key-to-tape entry with fifteen entry stations, labor costs and the wide fluctuations in seasonality dictated that we also employ an optical scanning device. This would enable us to "read" documents mailed to subscribers and returned by them, such as invoices, renewals, and book promotions, directly into a magnetic tape.

Our team visited various companies that produced these scanning units, and we observed demonstrations at manufacturer showroom locations. We wanted a medium-sized scanner that could process about fifteen thousand documents each day, but could handle a peak load of forty thousand per day, as well. Although we were mainly interested in picking up only "key line" data of significant subscriber information, we also wanted the flexibility of a full-page reader in the event we decided to expand its use to include donor/recipients and industrial subscribers.

We wanted a competitively priced model, delivered within ninety days, with two-shift, on-call maintenance support. Although optical scanning is still in its infancy, there are some fifteen to twenty companies already in this business. We had to sort out three scanners that met our criteria, and then select the one we judged to be the best.

Again, we developed technical specifications that detailed the type of transaction; volume of each transaction by year and month; cost comparison of key entry versus scanner; seasonal characteristics; method of input; character recognition; performance capability; visual display option; scanning technique; technical support; error control; method of document handling; and purchase or rental price and maintenance charge.

Prospective manufacturers were invited to bid, and we made our selection. We now had image-processing capability with a competitively priced optical character reader.

On schedule, the computer key-entry units and scanner were placed in operation. Systems were designed, and software programs were prepared, tested, and debugged to handle input data entry; post office validity check; change of address (chadd); master record maintenance and updating; complaints and adjustments; printing of issue labels, invoices, renewals, new list promotions, and other promotions; donor/ recipients and morgue file run; and Christmas gift sales effort.

Philip Brach now had his computerized system that would enable the paperwork activities to keep pace with his dynamic editorial crew. However, the new system had only brought the "back room" up to the normal pace of the young, aggressive editors, writers, and roving reporters.

Led by hard-nosed Joe Lonegan, the editor-in-chief, the staff soon wanted demographic studies, list purge matrix, [5] marketing selection of names regression system, and other variants of computer techniques in order to gauge subscriber preferences and desires more accurately.

So, stoke up the furnaces and full speed ahead—*Graphic Sports News and Views* has just begun to move hell-bent-for-leather into another period of astronomical growth.

Thirty staid businessmen dressed in double-breasted suits sit in a circle on hard wooden benches, waiting, like the dogs in Pavlov's famous experiment, for a bell to sound. These men decide the price that people throughout the world will pay for copper, lead, and zinc.

The scene is the London Metal Exchange where twice daily a series of bells triggers twenty-five minutes of frenzied trading in these valuable metals. The exchange members buy and sell millions of tons of the metals every day and, concurrently, establish the market price of each. The sessions begin very slowly, with various traders tossing out a bid or offer figure, looking for a nibble. Since a fraction of a cent can mean thousands of dollars either way, each trader is cautious—not unlike a skillful boxer sizing up his opponent in the early rounds of a fight.

However, as the trading time period nears an end (ten minutes is allotted for copper, the same for lead, with five minutes for zinc), the crescendo of shouting voices sounds like

---

[5] List purge matrix is concerned with elimination of subscribers of questionable value for any number of reasons.

the fishmongers' cries on Dover Street. Bare-knuckle in-fighting takes place as a final offer is shouted across the room by a London Metals Company executive to a gentleman from Rhodesia; two men, three seats apart, are haggling about one-eighth of a cent on 400 tons for delivery from a mine in Chile; and three others are frantically negotiating the sale of a six-month supply of copper bars neatly stacked in a warehouse in Perth Amboy, New Jersey.

Each trader may deal with any of the other twenty-nine. So the bid and asking prices fly back and forth in all directions, while dapper young clerks standing behind each member accurately jot down any finalized transactions in little black books.

The primary purpose of this unusual activity is to enable a metals-producing company to buy or sell enough metal to maintain its desired "position." This position may be either long (surplus inventory) or short (low inventory), depending upon the strategy dictated by prevailing circumstances. Translated into more specific terms, a copper-mining interest, for example, will sell the amount of metal needed to keep its mines in Chile, Peru, or Zambia producing at a steady rate. However, should worldwide conditions shift to a favorable sellers' market, the company may elect to build an inventory position in order to engage in hopefully lucrative pricing speculation. Although many attempts have been made within the industry to maintain price stability in copper, it has always resisted control. Pricewise, copper has proven to be the most volatile base metal.

Ametal, Ltd. is one of the London Metal Exchange members, with international mining interests requiring constant surveillance. Its copper position must be current on a moment-to-moment, twenty-four hour a day basis. Not too many years ago, this complex task had finally outstripped the human capacity of its clerical staff, so it was decided to computerize the copper position report. This document would have to contain information on copper availability at a bonded warehouse, a smelter, a refinery, enroute aboard an ocean vessel or by other mode of transportation, at a secondary facility, or at an affiliated copper concern.

When I was called in by Ametal, Ltd. to make the study, I first requested copies of all position reports. To my surprise, there were so many variations of this material in written form that the reports filled an entire briefcase.

I had to make field trips to ore beds, smelters, and refineries to obtain information about all the connecting links in the system. Also, I contacted bonded warehouses, commercial clearing houses, and U.S. port-of-entry officials to gather other pieces of data. Finally, I held discussions with various London Metal Exchange members to develop a pattern of trading operations in terms of volatility and volume.

With this massive amount of transactional data, I was then able to design a computerized position reporting system. It took many months to develop the input data, the software package, and the report printouts. When it was completed, however, the system provided Ametal with significant and timely information on physical copper available in all markets (bonded, duty-free, concentrated in bond, and so forth) for sale in the U.S. market—in substance, it reported total copper availability. Then, from this total, deductions were made for any copper already allocated in either the foreign[6] or domestic market. After these net available figures, the computer report indicated the fire-refined copper (after all impurities have been removed) available at various refineries,[7] electro-refined[8] (another process operation in the production of copper), and general copper mine tonnage through London Metal Exchange trades.

As the totals of each category were computed, the data began to print out grand totals by familiar copper refinery and

[6] The foreign position included tonnage sold on future delivery over a six-month period under a Peruvian/Argentine trade agreement.

[7] Fire-refined position is determined on the basis of available casting capacity. Fire-refined metal is not produced for stock.

[8] Electro position is based on the maximum capacity of tankhouse production casting raw material.

other centers such as the United States, Africa, Hamburg, and the Peruvian port of Callao.[9] Then, it printed a string of figures across the last line that indicated "copper available everywhere."

One other facet of the copper market had to be computerized to fully integrate the entire systems configuration. This segment of the system involved the purchase of scrap copper to be mixed with virgin ore. The daily *New York Times* shows the quoted prices of grades No. 1 and No. 2 copper and of light copper. But behind these figures, buyers in a company like Ametal, Ltd. will argue, cajole, and curse scrap dealers in order to buy this precious commodity at the best price. This scrap is eventually trucked to the smelters where it is mixed with the proper proportions of virgin ore to form 99.4 percent pure, orange-hued copper ingots.

A computer-generated report was designed to calculate the transaction and tie back automatically to the copper position report. The scrap contract data consisted of detailed information such as description of material (No. 1, No. 2, or light copper), settlement assay, net assay (after adjustment for moisture), metal allowance, dry weight, payable price and basis, and the margin amount (in dollars).

Speed was a critical consideration. The entire scrap-purchasing system was completely integrated so that when a customer order, cable, letter, or phone call was received, a sales contract could be prepared on tape and the data automatically transmitted to the computer facility.

On the other side of the world, a freighter loaded with copper ore from Zaire (formerly the Congo) may be plowing slowly through the waters of the South Atlantic Ocean en route to its destination in Antwerp, Belgium, with six days remaining on its voyage. But while its captain smokes his pipe and charts the course, thirty men in faraway London will be deciding who will own the ship's precious cargo when it arrives.

---

[9] The data covered consignment ships sailing on certain dates from the port of Callao.

9
Red Dog

Business is a game of numbers. What separates the successful businessman from one who fails is only a score of percentage points. Most executive managements would do handsprings if they could turn in profits just above the industry average.

Overall, the total business community is presently averaging a profit of about 5 percent after tax earnings. How many companies would settle for a 6 to 8 percent profit? The majority would. On the other hand, should a company experience losses averaging 3 to 5 percent for a few years, the executive revolving door would be whisking out the incumbents and bringing in a new team. So the spread between very good performance and catastrophe is only about 10 percent. It's not much when you consider that most other "games" are won or lost by lopsided scores.

Now let's go on to an analysis of the difference between greatness and mediocrity in management. What is the ingredient that separates the men from the boys? Surprisingly, it is *not* complex.

Excellent management occurs where the executives are pros who operate a business like any other professional undertaking. They do everything with meticulous precision, administrative skill, and the application of seasoned experience. Nothing is left to chance. Each area of expertise is competently staffed; executives are allowed to make decisions on their own and have subordinates capable of carrying out those decisions.

Conversely, poor management is found in those unfortunate companies run by men who cannot make a decision without consulting a horde of "rubber stamp" junior executives, and who lack the ability to distinguish between good and bad performances. In this environment, politics flourish like the wild jungle growth of the Brazilian tropics. Men are judged on a personal basis rather than on proven accomplishments.

Let's look at a typical business enterprise. It has a product or service to sell and, except for certain industries (drug) or companies (Xerox, Du Pont, IBM) that have proprietary items or patents, it must compete with other similar concerns in the marketplace. True, some firms make it for a while on personal contacts and interlocking directorates but, again, the vast majority of companies must give the customer value and service if they wish to prosper.

Within an industry, then, what makes for success? The answer is professional management. The man at the top makes the difference.

There is an old racetrack saying, "Bet the jockey." Why? Because the horse is the constant factor; the skilled jockey is the variable that makes it a race.

Essentially, every company must do the same basic things—buy raw materials, process them, and sell a product with some value added. Each organization has similar functions with which to carry out these activities. The primary requisite of management is to master thoroughly the fundamentals needed to run a business. In football, concentration on blocking and tackling comes before running, passing, or calling signals. The game doesn't start on the first play or in the huddle—it starts in hard contact scrimmages and long strategy meetings. Learning how to execute plays precedes actions (although this statement isn't meant to infer that the game is won in the coach's conference room.)

A company must begin with a tight cost control system, realistic budgets, sound planning, an effective production control system, responsive inventory controls, astute financial controls, an aggressive and imaginative marketing organization, competent and intelligent engineering activity, and a smooth-running manufacturing facility.

Executive management must have the ability to systematically organize each business function, staff departments with experienced personnel, and instill confidence and enthusiasm throughout the ranks of employees. From this sound rockbed of strength, the company can then develop secondary professional management skills in operations research, computerized data processing applications, management information systems, pure research and development, warehouse distribution and logistics, strategic business planning, optimization of resource allocation, acquisitions and mergers, and cash flow management.

In order to accomplish these objectives, a company must be adept at management development and organizational planning. These skills, in turn, require that the proper personnel be available, when needed, possessing a combination of aptitudes and personality traits that will mesh harmoniously and effectively.

People tend to pick people like themselves—and therein lies the rub. How can a person be objective in appraising another individual's talents if, at the same time, he wants to maintain a comfortable relationship with that individual?

Some good examples of the attraction of like personalities can be seen in the associates selected by recent chief executive officers of the United States. President Truman had his Kitchen Cabinet of card-playing cronies. Eisenhower relied on a few military acquaintances and other closely nourished friendships. The youthful Jack Kennedy was most at ease with his "Irish Mafia" and Harvard clique, while Lyndon Johnson had his ten-gallon-hat Texans. President Nixon, as might be expected, installed in high office relatively drab, middle-of-the-road businessmen and lawyers.

The head man selects his team and sets policy, and you better believe it! Knowing the characteristics of the head man provides insight into how his company operates.

A chief executive officer who is introspective and fair can learn a great deal about his organization by "looking in a mirror," since the company is an exact reflection of his own personality. His strengths and weaknesses permeate the entire chain of command. Occasionally, an individual survives who doesn't fit the corporate mold. But such mavericks stand out by their nonconformance and rarely make it to the top.

There is a card game called Red Dog. It's also a gambling game. Unlike poker, pinochle, or hearts, in Red Dog each person plays his hand alone instead of against the others.

Suppose you are the chief executive officer of the ABC Widget Corporation. Let's simulate a Red Dog game to show how your company may be vulnerable to competition—and in need of management development and organization planning.

Here's how the game works: At the outset, each player puts a few dollars into the pot. The cards are then dealt in sequence with the man to the dealer's left getting four cards with the next card placed face down. The object of the game is simple enough. The player must decide two things: whether or not he can beat the hidden card with one of his in the same suit, and how much to bet against the pot on his chances. Should he luckily draw a mixture of aces and high picture cards, he will no doubt gamble a substantial amount. Conversely, low cards, or all of one suit, would call for only a token wager.

The uncertainty and suspense in anticipating what the hole card is makes for a wild and woolly game. Though the contest appears to be an even one, at the end of the evening the pot is usually the winner. Most of the chips are scattered in disarray in the center of the table.

What does Red Dog have to do with the world of business? Let's continue and see. In industry, there are four major functions: engineering, marketing, manufacturing, and finance. Suppose we were to assign a suit to each of these functions and play this hypothetical Red Dog game with the stakes your company and the face-down card the competition ready to capitalize on your internal weaknesses.

Ready, Mr. Chief Executive Officer? Let's deal the cards and see how your corporation stacks up in this encounter. Our card lineup will play like this:

> engineering: spades
> marketing: clubs
> manufacturing: hearts
> finance: diamonds

The first card you look at in your hand is the queen of clubs. Not a bad draw but, after all, marketing is where you had years of solid experience and proven accomplishments— starting as a sales trainee, and twenty-eight years later moving directly from marketing vice-president to president.

Ah, here's the corner of a spade. That's the engineering card. With your degree in liberal arts and no postgraduate work, your only elbow-rubbing experience was in product development, so that would give you—there's the card—only a mediocre six of spades.

Manufacturing! Oil and water. Ever since your days as a raw recruit in the field, you've gone through many a customer wringer on late deliveries, unrealistic promise dates, stock-outs, and terrible service support. Yes, that card had to be low—a four of hearts.

Now finance is somewhat different! The board of directors drives you unmercifully, demanding better results in profits, sales, return on investment, research and development, and so on. So in this function, you'd better do your homework or you'll get boiled alive. Each month the "early warning" flash report reaches you on the second working day. However, the real test comes when the monthly profit and loss statement is brought to your office.

Let's see what the statement says: "Sales are off 6 percent against last year's comparable period and 14 percent against plan. Inventories are still increasing, despite controls that were supposed to have been installed last month. That damn ratio of overhead to direct labor is killing us on costs. When will the plant in Alabama fully absorb start-up expenses? How can *all* operating divisions show a bad quarter at the same time?"

"Miss Jones," you shout, "get my staff together for a meeting in the conference room in ten minutes." All hell's going to break loose today!

For services rendered above and beyond the call of duty, we'll award you a nine of diamonds for the finance card.

In our hypothetical Red Dog game, you, as the chief executive officer, had a queen, six, four, and nine. How much would the real you bet on these weak cards against the one face down? Maybe fifty cents or a buck, if you're a gambler. But why be such a piker when a bona fide corporation might bet $50,000, or $500,000, or perhaps $5 million on each major decision made by the person in charge?

Our Red Dog game indicates that probably "average" competition (the hole card) would have trounced this company in engineering, manufacturing, and possibly finance. Had the competitor been an astute professional like Tom Watson, Roy Little, or Harold Geneen, this company's chief executive would have required the strongest possible hand, consisting of an assortment of one-eyed jacks, ladies of the court, a king or two, and at least the ace of spades to stand a chance of winning the game.

What is the point of this exercise? As the Chinese proverb says, "One picture is worth more than ten thousand words." Red Dog is almost shocking in its simplicity. We all play cards. We all know which cards are higher than others. If a chief executive officer will admit to his company's structural weaknesses, he has already taken the first step toward building an effective organization of broad-gauged, competent executives.

What can be done to move off dead center? Start by recognizing that because of the way most industrial concerns are organized, executives advance within one functional expertise. We live in the age of specialization of talents. If education, training, and experience have any market value (and I strongly believe they do), then a man will tend to stay in his proven field because his company benefits most by it and he feels confident in his job.

However, the chief executive officer must plan the progression that his key men will take, starting with the first management positions they held. Either by the C.E.O. or through an experienced executive management development training officer, each person should have a master career blueprint spelled out in detail, with indications of areas where personal development is required. A company should invest in its human resources in the same way that it invests in machine tools, plant facilities, and materials.

First, the management candidate, whom we shall call Joe Smith, should be thoroughly tested for basic intelligence, personality traits, and general interests. How far can he go and in what direction? Qualified company executives should meet with Joe and discuss frankly what the future portends at that point in his career. This discussion would cover building a solid base in such job prerequisites as verbal and written communications, human behavior and human relations, motivation and morale, understanding of corporate policies and procedures, labor relations, work habits and attitude, confidence and poise, leadership qualities, and basic work content.

With Joe's cooperation, the company should then design a program tailor-made for him, to assist him in developing most of these skills. The program may extend over as many as five years, and Joe should be continually guided and counseled along the way until he becomes self-sufficient.

Each Joe will require a different program. Some individuals will need more formal training—books, courses, seminars, meetings. Others may need more subtle types of development—public speaking, English, liberal arts, human relations. Each man should feel that his long-term program will mold his character and personality and help him become a flexible, outgoing, intelligent, confident human being.

After he progresses through this basic developmental period, Joe should be capable of moving into a middle management position. His growth should continue on a planned basis but, in addition, he should now become a member of a management team that holds formal meetings periodically. The men of this middle management team will be working together to make the enterprise more successful, and the team members should always be available and willing to discuss problems individually or collectively.

While working with middle management, Joe should be exposed to other organizational areas. He should begin to learn about sales, production, personnel, procurement, accounting, traffic, materials management, distribution, product engineering, and computer applications. Concurrently, either in local colleges or through company training classes, he should continue to take courses that include conceptual thinking, logic, and applied reasoning.

Now that he is a solid individual with basic knowledge and at least one functional area of competence, Joe should be ready to be rotated into other functional areas. Normally he should be assigned to positions that have some common relationship to his previous job. The duties should be homogeneous—a good mix. Joe should be prepared to handle the assignments, since he has been exposed to each new job through the management meetings, informal bull sessions, courses, and personal guidance.

When he moves into each new assignment, Joe will need constructive suggestions, not wanton criticism. His responsibilities should be in accord with his experience. Most of the routine work should be handled by departmental personnel. Joe should become involved in only one segment of the job initially, but in depth. He should do everything that is required in the job, including the detailed portion, when he can master it.

Over a period of time, Joe will gradually develop the capabilities needed to do the work in a professional manner. He can then be measured on his performance during each stage of this developmental process, and on his ability to motivate and lead other people. No excuses can be given that Joe was unprepared for the assignment. Or, as one chief executive quite candidly told me, "I moved up to this position because I was no good at anything else and therefore expendable."

After a number of years of planned rotation involving at least two of the four major functions (and a few secondary ones as well), Joe should be ready to assume executive status. An executive management committee will begin to invite him to participate in their periodic meetings. Again, through formal and informal training and development, Joe should begin to appreciate the overview approach to high-level decision making. He should now be prepared to exercise quality judgments, thanks to his years of sound experience and development.

Although he will make some mistakes, Joe's batting average should be consistently better than that of his opposition. He is now playing picture cards against the deuces and threes of his competitors. Within a reasonable period of time, he should be ready to become a senior executive officer of the corporation.

What was the total cost, to the company, of Joe's training? Negative! Without a management development program, a business leaves itself open to incompetence, executive turnover, infighting, and politics, which are the friction that slows down most companies. By following this systematic approach to management development, a company gets a real bargain—a Hot Dog, as we say in the trade, a real Red (Hot) Dog.

Parker Pulp and Paper spread its corporate body over thousands of acres of prime woodland, from the snow-packed mountains of Maine spruce to tracts of spindle-shaped pine trees sprawled across central Florida. Culling trees from these vast holdings, the company was able to chop them into manageable logs; remove the bark; cut the logs into chips; chemically cook the chips into a pulp; fluff up the pulp with air at high pressure; run the pulp through a mixing box; and then send the wet mass through a football-field-length drier where it becomes paper and is dried and thinned by a steam-heated rolling process into the final thickness, is calendered, and wound into a large roll.

Once the process was completed, Parker could then elect either to sell the large, jumbo roll or use it to produce paper for bags, sacks, wrapping, and printing, and paperboard for containers, cartons, and boxes. Or it could also make bags of multiwall construction for fertilizer or produce toilet tissue, disposable diapers, and other consumer products.

Parker Pulp and Paper had recently installed a mammoth facility in Martinsville, Florida, just forty miles from Disney World. A steady stream of management people was needed to run the plant, coordinate operations from headquarters in New York, and develop marketing and product strategies to optimize profits on plant yield.

James Connaughton, a former federal labor mediator, was vice-president of personnel administration for Parker. He recognized the need to provide current and future managerial talent at all levels in the organization. I was just completing a data processing installation, tying in corporate order processing and scheduling with production control at the Martinsville plant, when Connaughton invited me into his paneled office in New York.

"Jerry," he began, "we're going to be in deep trouble if we don't get moving fast on planning our organizational requirements and setting up a management training and development program. That place in Martinsville is straining our capacity to fill key management positions both here and down south. Can you begin work on this problem so that we can make inroads on it within a realistic time span?"

I knew the people in the company and I had visited Parker facilities in Maine, New Hampshire, and Florida while developing the data processing system. It seemed to me that the most productive method for me to follow would be to do forward planning on the basis of position grades where jobs of equal value could be grouped together. I needed personnel statistics, since the future is a reflection on past occurrences, factored for any unusual changes.

I asked Connaughton to provide figures on the severance ratio and plotted it for the past few years. The information came from W-2 forms that indicated the percentage of employees who quit or were dismissed. Peaks and valleys in employment levels were analyzed as to cause.

Next, I developed death and disability ratios. What percentage of the management people were involved in these unfortunate events? Then I tackled the easy one—working out Parker's retirement ratio. Since the company had a mandatory retirement policy, this information was readily available. Terminations, deaths, and retirements—a composite of the three gave me the severance ratio. This told me how many employees should be hired just to keep a static work force.

Now came the toughest group of figures—the promotion ratio. How many employees would be promoted during each year as a result of the vacancies created by severance?

Armed with these basic statistics, I then met with Connaughton and other Parker executives to obtain projections of where the company could be expected to be in one year, in five years, or in whatever periods were considered important to company plans.

I asked many soul-searching questions in these sessions. What are your market forecasts? What are your product forecasts? What are your plant and facility forecasts?

These forecasts were broken down in periods to correspond

with financial and physical resource planning needs. I was then able to determine the kind of manpower needed, by manpower category. We then constructed a promotability chart that showed where the management force could come from within the organization, and where we needed outside recruitment.

This chart listed every man in the management and professional organization. Each key employee was listed according to position, position grade, and location. We used a codified system to detail pertinent statistical information and a color code system to indicate degree of promotability. The same chart was used to anticipate requirements in advance.

Next, we had to accelerate the developmental process in order to prepare more people for positions in Martinsville; Dewhurst, Maine; Brendenwood, New Hampshire; and at headquarters in New York.

How do management and professional people develop?

Unfortunately, not by taking canned courses. Most growth is attributable to on-the-job development, either from self-training, training by the immediate supervisor, or training by fellow employees in the same or similar functions.

The project took time. The management development program lasted a number of months and consisted mainly of a case-method approach. Material was prepared from actual company situations covering: warehouse inventory control; evaluation of private brands versus company branded products; research and development of disposable undergarments; pricing policy for jobbers and chain stores; plant loading through computerized operations research techniques; bag and sack inventory position analyses; cost control for converting operation; moving merchant sales function to Martinsville; executive sales strategy; credit and collection policies and procedures; and a total management information reporting system.

Trees take years to grow and so, too, do people. Neither can be force-fed with any degree of success in order to speed up the growth process. But once the pipeline started to fill up with forward-looking, fast-acting people, the Parker Pulp and Paper Company could be assured of a dynamic future.

Sometimes development is generated on an ad hoc basis by people themselves, rather than through company sponsorship. This is an excellent means for improving the calibre of talent because it is fully supported by the participants. A firm can provide the meeting place and offer speakers or conference guests, as the group desires. But the members of the group should decide the format of the program, the selection of the guest speakers, the timing of the meetings, and who will be included in the group.

After I had fulfilled a number of consulting assignments at Weldon Chemicals in Wyandotte, Michigan, I was asked by a contingent of youthful, lower- and middle-level staff and professional people in the company to aid in getting a program of this type started. With management's wholehearted endorsement of the concept, the group arranged to meet every other week in a downtown club. Meetings were informal and often lasted until almost midnight. Guest speakers were encouraged to talk extemporaneously on their topics. The group adopted a no-holds-barred approach in milking the speaker for every drop of his knowledge.

One session got rather heated when a top steel executive claimed that organizations are too confining and that people should move into the gray areas between organization blocks unilaterally, as the need for decisive action so dictates. A panel of three Detroit-based purchasing executives explained how to negotiate contracts, select vendors, obtain blanket orders, and handle the basic procurement function. It required two highly technical meetings for the head of research and development of an electronics company to cover all the products of a non-confidential nature on the company's drawing board.

Computers got their day in court through in-depth presentations by hardware manufacturer specialists. Similarly, the topics of systems design, forms control, and records management received clear and concise definition through exploration by vendor representatives proficient in each of these areas. Local business leaders spoke on finance, cost accounting, cash management, corporate planning, and acquisitions and mergers.

People hunger for knowledge—particularly the youthful, up-and-coming junior executives. It's no wonder they become frustrated and disillusioned when asked to work in a mental vacuum. Far too few individuals in executive management understand fully this need of junior personnel for job fulfillment and job enrichment. But the wives and children of these junior executives, who know first-hand their anguish, can attest to the years wasted while their minds lay fallow, waiting for the company to exploit this latent depository of unused gray matter.

10
Topsy Never Made It Big

Most companies grow like Topsy, carried along by a hard-driving entrepreneur, an inventive genius, a unique product, good timing, or sheer luck. But few of these make the big time without sound planning. As J. Walter Garvey, board chairman of Steelco, said when he took over the helm and began to plot a successful course of action for the company, "The time has come to think before you act, and then act decisively." No longer could Steelco fly by the seat of its pants and get by. It was now expected to meet a commitment of steady growth and profitability.

Garvey recognized the magnitude of his task since the company had sales of $180 million—with the potential to be twice that size. So with board approval, I was engaged to assist in the development of a soundly structured planning program for the corporation.

Our first formal meeting was in Garvey's teak-paneled office on the twenty-sixth floor of a modern steel structure, one block removed from New York's Rockefeller Center. As I entered, he motioned toward a comfortable grouping around an antique Louis XIV table, so that we could speak in a relaxed atmosphere.

Garvey was athletically proportioned, with an imposing six-foot-four-inch frame. His slightly gray hair and neatly trimmed black mustache blended well with the charcoal-colored, hand-blocked foulard necktie and his immaculately tailored black pinstripe suit. His walking cane stood erect near the door, ready for his departure to Greenwich, Connecticut, promptly at 6:15 P.M.

We spoke for over forty minutes about the complexities of the assignment and the impact it would have on the organization. As we visualized the change, it would completely restructure a disorganized operation and transform it into one that would demand disciplined planning and objective measurement of management's performance. The controls that would be established would indicate the people who could accept responsibility and those who could not.

Garvey and I agreed that planning must begin with a clear definition of company objectives and explicit executive management policy statements. We took note of the fact that as a business grows, the very size of the operation diminishes the original close contact and communications that had existed between its various people.

Since many important decisions were being made each day in all parts of the Steelco operation, we recognized that it would be imperative to devise a means whereby these decisions would be consistent with the aims of the chief executive officer. This concept would have to be an essential component of the planning mechanism if all levels of management were to have the freedom and confidence needed to move in the proper direction—and together.

After this meeting, I spent a number of weeks doing intensive research, learning the composition of each organizational component of the company. The information I gleaned during this fact-finding mission indicated that Steelco, as a widely diversified manufacturing enterprise, should be structured along divisional lines. This reorganization would be a logical step toward providing the solid base needed to expand sales and increase profits in each diversified branch of the company. It would enable executive management to place complete accountability in the hands of a selected group of competent division general managers.

However, Garvey was also concerned with the possibility of his losing control of the entire enterprise through the tendency of independent divisions to become fully autonomous under remote control management. Therefore, it would be necessary to institute positive controls, with a reliable monitoring device, within the framework of the planning process. If this were done, the program would provide executive management with division plans and goals, the means to measure results periodically, and the ability to counteract any significant departure from the basic plan.

Previously, Steelco had operated on a committee basis. Members of an executive committee met regularly to discuss various matters and arrive at policy decisions. It was a slow-moving procedure and important decisions were deferred almost indefinitely. Compromises and concessions ultimately watered down most agreements. Accountability became vague and uncertain.

The company lacked a tight budgetary control system, reliable cost accounting data, and clearly defined short- and long-range performance goals.

The plants were hampered by outmoded production methods and had never been held accountable as cost centers for direct operating expense chargeable to their respective departments.

Financial reports were so voluminous that they were never completely understood or fully utilized. Capital expenditures were inconsistent with financial and marketing needs; as a result, many ventures became speculative efforts rather than soundly conceived programs.

The initial phase of the reorganization program involved the development of plans for each segment of the business by the appropriate executive. Because of the duration of the business cycle and the time frame for capital formation in the steel industry, long-range planning extended over a period of ten years.

The corporate president, Raymond Reinhardt, was charged with the responsibility of reviewing and approving the division plans.

After the plans were defined, the corporate controller, Fred Staal, audited them, giving particular emphasis to assumptions, significant factors (variables), and financial adequacy.

Next, a timetable was prepared to coordinate the preparation and submission of profit plans. At this point, general economic forecast data were included in order to project events that might have a bearing on the long-range plan over the ten-year period. These data included forecasts of the construction industry, and of automotive, appliance, and other end-users of Steelco products, both domestic and foreign.

The plan established specific objectives, such as achieving a certain return on invested capital or capturing a particular share of the market. The objectives were not necessarily all quantitative; they included such qualitative factors as industry reputation and quality of service to customers.

Also, assumptions and suppositions regarding economic conditions, changes in pricing, and other internal and external factors were considered, inasmuch as they affected long-range planning.

We recognized that assumptions might involve conditions beyond the control of the individuals concerned. Nevertheless, we believed that they served as a much needed supplement to fortify available factual data.

The plan had to be executed throughout the entire organization. After reviewing the program and satisfying himself that it accomplished its purpose, Garvey drafted a letter of transmittal that contained a statement of general corporate aims, an economic prediction, and a summary of the program.

The summary was focused on the following:

1. The projected effect of changes on the business, with consideration given to such external factors as growth of the economy, competition, and levels of customer requirements.
2. The projected effect of special internal programs such as new facilities, new products currently in process, and products or services in the planning stage.
3. The capital requirements of the business.
4. The trend in earnings.
5. A statement of programs.
6. A statement of key factors (variables) and assumptions.
7. Appropriate financial statements.
8. A summary of capital expenditures.
9. Other data such as industry projections and manpower requirements.

Finally, all supporting financial reports and operating procedures were developed. These included material on sales, capital appropriations, labor and materials cost, administrative expense figures, and other pertinent financial data. These reports also contained information on division goals, strategies, and contingency programs for recovering from a deviation from plan.

The program was implemented. Steelco witnessed improvement in its operating performance, thanks to the planning and controls initiated by Garvey and Reinhardt.

In retrospect, I realized that a few managers played the numbers game and intentionally hedged their forecasts, while others were either too cautious or overly optimistic. But in these instances, executive management understood each person's idiosyncracies, and allowed for some degree of flexibility to adjust to the individual. Management reasoned that it would be shortsighted to accept an individual's unrealistic targets and then dismiss him for his failure to meet expectations or to remain within an acceptable variance of plan.

An example may serve to illustrate this point. A prominent aerospace company, with which I had been active in another capacity, instituted profit center accountability. All thirty-five profit center heads planned at least a 20 percent increase in sales volume—because that's what the executive vice-president expected of them. Only two achieved this goal. Most of the others attained an acceptable sales growth of 5 to 8 percent, while a few showed a loss. Because they fell below target, a number of these managers were replaced. What was gained by this unreasonable demand to achieve the unattainable?

Consolidated Petroleum is a worldwide, $600 million oil and natural gas company. Its management was interested in a short- and long-range planning program.

My evaluation of the company and the industry led me to suggest structuring the program on the basis of one to five years as short-term and fifteen years for long-term, because natural resource ventures involving initial exploration, capitalization, and start-up may extend over many years.

Short-range planning segmented into these major elements:

1. A company yearly profit plan, including forecast balance sheets and return on assets for each of the company's divisions.
2. Operating budgets that are used to develop these profit plans.
3. A monthly profit and working capital forecast.

At Consolidated, management people had to be made knowledgeable in the technique of profit planning. Short-range planning is more understandable, since it contains relatively reliable data. But long-range planning, with its many unknowns and variables, is still an art—much like the field of economics.

I worked closely with Winthrop Troy, vice-president of finance, in preparing material for use in training Consolidated's management personnel.

At the training sessions, I emphasized that the basic philosophy underlying the profit plan—and the cost price and volume assumptions upon which it was based—was as follows:

1. The profit plan and subsidiary budgets represented each executive's considered judgment on what he planned to achieve in the period covered. In addition, it was expected that the profit plan and operating budgets for each division would show an improvement each year over the previous year, unless major economic conditions beyond the control of the executive made this impossible.
2. However, attainment of the plan was not, in itself, to be considered satisfactory performance; and, conversely, failure to achieve the plan was not necessarily unsatisfactory performance. Rather, the plan was to be regarded as a base of reference against which explanations for favorable and unfavorable variances from plan would be required.

As the training program continued, we further defined the approach and philosophy of profit planning.

Comparisons with the previous year's actual results were to be made only at the time the plan was being prepared. Once the plan was agreed upon by all Consolidated Petroleum executives, no further comparisons were to be made. Comparisons of the profit plan would then be judged against current year actuals—with reasons for the differences explained in terms of price, volume, cost, and product mix. Comparative data would also be used to compare Consolidated against other companies in the industry. These evaluations would be made on such factors as return on assets, margin on sales, inventory turnaround, ratio of supervision to direct labor, and other significant yardsticks.

Once the management people were thoroughly in-
doctrinated in the planning process, it was then possible for
Consolidated to complete the design of a system tailored to its
exacting requirements. Within a few months, the company
had developed a nucleus of in-house talent capable of instituting a planning and control function.

Consolidated Petroleum was now prepared to develop its
future plans in a professional manner. In an industry where
stakes are high, today's decision may have tremendous impact
on future earnings.

Pantyhose beat the pants off hosiery and garter belts. In
fact, it was no contest. Back in the mid-1960s, women began
to realize that pantyhose were much more comfortable, and
less revealing, than a pair of stockings—and the craze was on.
Garter belts went the way of the buggy whip.

Soon the U.S. market was flooded with foreign imports.
German manufacturers moved aggressively into supermarkets
and other mass distribution channels. Although their pantyhose had too much material at the ankles—they were
patterned upon the typical German Hausfrau shape—the
price was right and the merchandise moved off the shelves.
The Japanese were right behind the Germans with pantyhose
that could be sold through discount outlets and lower-priced
department stores. Most American women never realized that
the reason they had to tug their pantyhose up every so often
was because they were patterned to fit the smaller-framed,
shorter-legged Japanese woman.

Slimfit had been in the hosiery manufacturing business for
fifteen years. It did extremely well in satisfying consumer
demand for pantyhose when the market was growing by leaps
and bounds. But now, with the inroads of imported merchandise and the stiffening competitive posture of the large
U.S. hosiery producers, Slimfit was beginning to feel the
pinch. Pricing had become fierce and, unless it began to
operate professionally, Slimfit faced the threat of a serious

erosion of its business. Accordingly, the company had to reassess its position and develop a plan that would provide it with a more secure niche in the industry.

Stanley Silvers ran his company from the Empire State Building, which is the hub of the New York City hosiery industry. He had surveyed the situation besetting the industry and realized that something had to be done to protect his investment. Through a mutual friend, he contacted me and sought advice.

My office, then located on Madison Avenue at Fortieth Street, was less than twenty minutes from Slimfit's headquarters. Within one hour after Silvers called, I had walked the distance and taken the two banks of elevators required to reach his floor. Finding his suite, I glanced quickly at the list of subsidiary company names printed in bold gold lettering on the door. The suite consisted of a reception area, a large general office, and three smaller private offices located on the perimeter of the building.

Silvers greeted me warmly. His silver-thatched hair and sideburns expressed more fully his identity than did his surname. He invited me into his comfortable office and immediately began to discuss the problem.

"Mr. Fuchs, the market is collapsing. There is a price war going on, and I can be squeezed out of business unless I am smarter than my competition. I must learn how to plan and operate my business in a professional manner or I'll be kaput. Fortunately, I have enough capital and following in the trade to weather this thing without panicking."

Stanley's son, Marvin, had now joined our discussion, and he nodded his head in agreement. I learned later that Marvin had had three years of business schooling at Columbia University, and it was he who had actually prodded his father into calling in a consultant.

At the conclusion of the meeting, the three of us agreed that the first step would be a fact-finding trip to each location and a gathering of industry and market data. Stanley and I would make the swing to the various plants, while Marvin would obtain all relevant material.

Two weeks later, we met again in Stanley's office, prepared to establish a formal planning program.

Slimfit was an unbranded manufacturer. We decided that the company should become both a branded and private label source of supply for chains, individual retailers, department stores, specialty shops, and hosiery stores; and occasionally—when liquidity might be needed—it should sell to rack jobbers and wholesalers.

The plan we devised would concentrate the company's energies toward expanding the private label market. It was expected that about 30 percent of total company sales would be achieved from this market. Business would be obtained from large food, apparel, and drug chains, and from major department stores. Concurrently, Slimfit would obtain selected rack jobbers to become involved in the company's brand label marketing program to facilitate entry into that segment of the market.

The plan envisioned that while private label business would be increasing as a percentage of total sales, the less profitable unbranded and wholesale market segments would diminish accordingly. Unbranded items were primarily channeled through shoe chains, or they were used as promotional goods and sold to the same outlets at a lower price for specials and promotions. Wholesalers were sold private labels for distribution through jobbers, who in turn sell to discount outlets and chain stores at low profit margins.

The second stage of the plan called for the company to market its Slimfit label to specialty stores, hosiery stores, small accounts, and department stores. The data Marvin had collected on previous sales indicated that the Slimfit label could compete favorably on price with the major pantyhose manufacturers, with equivalent quality and service. We estimated that the Slimfit label could account for 10 percent of total company sales by the following year and approach 20 percent the second year.

The carefully developed plan provided for continued growth in the private label segment, reaching 45 percent in the next year and leveling off at about 60 percent of company sales thereafter. This increase would be achieved at the expense of unbranded items, which would be expected to drop to 20 percent of total sales volume during this period, and of wholesalers, who would be virtually eliminated as Slimfit customers.

Marketing strategies were hammered out with Lou Gershon, the sales manager, his salesmen, and sales representatives. Major accounts in New York and California would be maintained by Stanley Silvers, while Lou Gershon would handle all major accounts in Chicago, Washington, D.C., Baltimore, Boston, and Ohio. Sales territories that involved New Jersey, New England, Texas, and Oklahoma–were carefully parceled out to the salesmen and sales representatives to achieve optimum sales penetration. Each territory was broken down by potential sales within market type, key account potential, and forecast for the balance of the business.

It was planned that two additional salesmen would be needed in the next twelve months to cover other areas in California and Michigan. It was estimated that their contribution would add between 5 and 8 percent to total company sales. A year later another salesman would be added to cover New York State and Pennsylvania, bringing in another 3 to 5 percent of business.

During this transition, Stanley Silvers would reduce his selling work load proportionately and devote more time to administrative matters, planning, and marketing.

Developing the plan further, we determined that the Slimfit company brand would be introduced with a complete marketing program. This program would include display racks, literature, and other rack-jobber salesmen aids provided by the company. Delivery of replenishment merchandise would be done automatically, using the split ticket method.

The Slimfit label would consist of five basic styles: one size, three size, three-size opaque, outsize, and stretch stocking.

The salesmen would carry and sell merchandise on a guaranteed sale arrangement.

Merchandise would retail from $1.69 to $2.49 each.

Salesmen would be trained to stress fit and constructiton in order to create a quality image, similar to competitors such as Fruit of the Loom, Kaiser-Roth, and Burlington.

Customers would be small drugstores, grocery stores, cigar stores, candy stores, and others, on a "locker stock" concept.[10] This would provide complete protection of replenishment stock to the stores through the maintenance of inventory controls by the company salesmen.

The company would provide an initial inventory of 2,000 dozen pantyhose at cost in the jobber's warehouse.

The plan called for the company to sell merchandise to rack jobbers at $1.50 to $2.00 per dozen below competition. Average selling price to the jobber would be between $6.75 and $10.50 per dozen.

Private label merchandise would be sold in the following styles: one size (fits all), three size—small, medium, and large—(multifilament), outsize, opaque, non-run, all nude, stretch, and knee-high.

Sales would be made to chains and department stores based primarily on price.

The company would promote services such as split ticket inventory control method, quick delivery, and back-up stock.

Jobbers would be phased out and used only for close-outs and overproduction.

Unbranded merchandise would be handled through broad-sized, mail-order circulation to old accounts on prepackaged dump display, or through promotion in variety stores.

In conjunction with the marketing plan, we also developed manufacturing support. The mill in Massachusetts was placed under tighter quality control procedures. Every shipment of

---

[10] The locker stock concept refers to a method of constantly providing backup stock to a store to maintain satisfactory store inventory.

greige goods[11] from the mill to the manufacturing plant in eastern Pennsylvania was inspected for fit and conformance to rigid quality control standards. With full machine utilization, on a three-shift basis, the mill could produce at a cost of $2.50 to $2.65 per dozen. This cost would enable us to push forward on the rack-jobber marketing program with assurance that a satisfactory profit margin could be achieved.

At the manufacturing plant, where the greige goods are dyed, finished, and packaged, the plan called for a reduction in costs from $1.10 per dozen to $1.02 per dozen during the current year. Marvin Silvers was given the assignment to execute this part of the program.

A new slitting machine was installed that brought production on this operation from 230 units per day to 350. An automatic dump machine was purchased to increase the speed of the bagging operation. A production control system was developed to control preproduction requirements, packaging supplies, greige goods, and other basic items.

The plant needed an improved cost accounting system. Working closely with Marvin Silvers, I designed a standard cost system that established incremental production levels of 12,000, 15,000, and 20,000 dozen per week for comparison against actual costs. The average shipments per week from manufacturing were 15,000 dozen, with the plan calling for proportionate increases in capacity in line with the marketing plan.

Financial planning was folded into the overall program based upon the assumption we had made. Profit plan figures were predicated on prices remaining within a range of $5.00 per dozen, on sales quotas being met, and on basic plant and mill methods improvements being achieved.

These financial considerations also anticipated that the Slimfit marketing program would be successfully introduced the first year, and that continued growth would occur in the private label market segment.

---

[11] Greige goods are knitted materials that have not yet been dyed.

Now, at last, Stanley Silvers had something concrete to use in competing with others in the industry. As he gazed out the window, his thoughts somehow drifted to another possibility. What would all of those specks of people walking along Fifth Avenue do if the mayor and his subordinates could plan the city's needs in the same manner? Certainly, the citizens of this great city would at least be reassured that the midtown traffic congestion might one day diminish, taxes might become stabilized, and crime might somehow be contained.

Then, suddenly, the smog rolled in, and Stanley Silvers shrugged his shoulders, turned from the window, and went back to work.

Profit planning is somewhat akin to organization planning. Both must be developed with sufficient flexibility to meet any contingency that might arise in a given circumstance. Although a uniform body of knowledge on the subject of planning is beginning to take shape, planning in itself should never become a constrictive device. Its purpose is to chart a course that someone can follow.

In fact, the art of successful planning is in the adherence to, and execution of, the plan.

A pilot will head for his destination with the aid of a flight plan. But a shift in wind direction or a change in wind velocity may require a deviation from the plan. The skilled pilot will tell you, "Make a three-degree or five-degree correction frequently if the plane is drifting off course, but *never* wait until a twenty-degree or thirty-degree change in direction is required." This reasoning is the hallmark of a well-managed company.

The appliance industry has unique characteristics that demand sound and effective planning decisions. KF Industries made refrigerators, vacuum cleaners, dishwashers, and clothes dryers. Each product line had varying competitive conditions, depending upon the strength of KF Industries' product identification, market penetration, and competitive strength in that particular market segment.

With the economy in its present state, the consumer is under pressure to judiciously weigh each buying decision. Austin Ambrose, president of KF Industries, decided to seek my aid in establishing a planning and control function which would assist executive management in formulating future profit objectives and would develop programs necessary to properly use all corporate assets in order to achieve the desired result.

In today's business language, the terms "planning" and "control" are sometimes thought to be synonymous. Actually, planning, without the means to control the fulfillment of the plan, soon loses any real significance. For this reason, Ambrose assigned the planning function to a top-level corporate vice-president who was responsible both for planning the short- and long-range goals and for following up to ensure that disciplined and coordinated actions would bring about the anticipated gains.

As I worked closely with Ambrose, with other senior executives, and with Logan Tracy, vice-president in charge of corporate planning, the planning elements began to take shape. They consisted of the following:

1. Financial planning
   a. Profit analysis
   b. Return on investment
   c. Property, plant, and equipment expenditures
   d. Acquisitions
   e. Inventory requirements
2. Marketing planning
   a. Economic indicators
   b. Government legislation and regulations
   c. Products and services
   d. Competitive elements
   e. Sales performance indicators

3. Personnel relations planning
   a. Executive development and key position requirements
   b. Total projected personnel needs
   c. Ratio of personnel to company sales
4. Production planning
   a. Projected raw material needs
   b. Projected production capabilities
   c. Projected labor requirements
5. Manufacturing planning
   a. Physical plant and machine tool needs
   b. New projects and construction budgets
   c. Space capacity and cost of existing facility
6. Research and development planning
   a. Technical programs and product opportunities
   b. Product research objectives
   c. Projected project costs
   d. Projected professional and staff needs

The KF Industries management decided that, to achieve effective planning, the newly created function should embody the total effort of all corporate operations. This did not mean that Logan Tracy and his people would usurp the authority and accountability of division managements. Rather, it meant that the company now had one group that could assimilate, digest, and evaluate problems and recommend a course of action predicated on known quantities and reasonable assumptions of future unknowns. Simply stated, the purpose of the new function was to "outplan" rather than "outguess" future business needs.

Control must, of necessity, overlap and be an integral adjunct to the planning activity. Therefore, we developed key elements of control in order to analyze the following factors:

1. Return on investment
2. Sales per employee

3. Ratio of administrative to direct production costs
4. Pricing history and trends
5. Price determinants
6. Profit margins at plant volumes and various price levels
7. Raw material determinants and trends
8. Break-even analysis
9. Volume and margin analysis
10. Economic and physical life of facilities
11. Current and future potential uses of products

KF Industries now had all the ingredients necessary to operate effectively. It could chart its course accurately and make minor, fine-tuning adjustments to its plan as changes in the marketplace, money market, or competitive conditions warranted. Ambrose and Tracy could constantly coordinate the various activities of the enterprise with confidence that the business would remain within an acceptable sales and profit band.

Some might say that there will always be a place for Topsy in the American scheme of things. Perhaps—but the company that turns on a dime year after year will eventually collapse from sheer exhaustion.

Planning provides management people with a mechanism to think things out and to respond to crises with appropriate action. It allows time to study and evaluate the current and foreseeable business climate, to determine the extent of modernization of facilities, to upgrade machine tools, to develop pricing policy, to consider market strategies, and to initiate new product development programs.

No sensible person expects planning to eliminate the old reliable crystal ball completely. At times, we all must rely on intuitive judgments. Planning does, however, cut down the odds so that a company has a better chance to make a reasonable profit. And after all, isn't profit the name of the game?

11
If You've Seen One,
You've Seen Them All

It was a hot, sultry afternoon in the city of Kaliganj located on India's Ganges River, one hundred and fifty miles upstream from where the river empties into the Bay of Bengal. Slowly a ferry loaded with its human cargo pulled away from the moorings, headed for Debharata ten miles to the north.

Suddenly, a fast riverboat came within 200 yards of the ferry. The mass of people aboard the ferry crowded to one side to cheer those in the fast boat. As dangerously sharp waves from the riverboat's backwash began to hit the ferry broadside, another boat passed by on its other side—and instinctively the ferry passengers darted to that side to shout and wave at those on the second vessel. At that precise moment, when the ferry was poised like a giant seesaw—with all the weight of the passengers on one side and the opposite side suspended high in the air—a huge wave flipped it over. About 300 men, women, and children drowned in this sorrowful incident on the Ganges.

I have never forgotten the tragedy that befell these people at Kaliganj because, in many respects, what they did to precipitate this incident is analogous to the actions of American businessmen. In general, executives in industry tend to make decisions that move them from one extreme of optimism or of pessimism to the other, according to the current economic conditions. When the business cycle is on the upturn, virtually all companies expand furiously with investments in plant facilities, machine tools, new products, and inventories. When this expansion policy has outstripped normal market growth, it's back to retrenchment with plant shutdowns, worker layoffs, curtailment of overtime, "make-to-order only," and sharp reductions in services and overhead costs. Then the economy, figuratively speaking, capsizes and sinks for a year or two until, once again, all company managements begin to gain enough confidence in the business climate to initiate another concerted upward movement in this never-ending chain of boom or bust cycles.

Within our free enterprise system, this problem may never be resolved. For when the money supply dries up, as a result of restrictive monetary and fiscal policies, industrial expansion is adversely affected. Then the economy must gradually reverse itself in order to recover lost ground and eventually gain sufficient momentum to stage a vigorous turnabout. However, it is possible for a company with a responsive organization to mitigate the impact of these external factors. Certainly, the test of effective management is the ability to navigate on a steady course through treacherous economic undercurrents—and remain relatively unscathed.

On the surface, companies appear to be structured differently. But in fact, most are either organized functionally along line and staff areas of responsibility or divisionalized with profit center accountability. This rigidity in format is tempered only by the personality of the individuals working for a company. The characteristics of its staff impart a semblance of uniqueness to an organization.

Basically, as far as industrial concerns go, if you've seen one, you've seen them all!

How, then, can a company stand apart from all others and function in a truly different internal environment? Simply by making the people masters of its organization, rather than the other way around. That's how Vortex Industries operates, and why it is successful in any economic climate.

I became involved with Vortex during an era of general prosperity. Although the company had grown rapidly, one cardinal rule that it had enforced was, "Never set unrealistic goals." To achieve this aim required precise knowledge of its customers and markets. A sophisticated planning and control system had been developed to serve this purpose.

Vortex management wisely accepted reality. In an industry with a 7 percent annualized growth rate, Vortex recognized that it would be foolhardy to project 20 to 25 percent growth and it established plans accordingly. Company officers reasoned that if they continually expected to expand by taking someone else's share of the market, the day would come when the guys holding the bag might very likely be themselves.

So Vortex Industries built its organization around missions and intermediate objectives and kept it tight and flexible. Specialists, skilled in narrow areas of expertise, were not placed on the payroll. Instead, Warren Kaiser, the president, used a few assistants for various assignments that were outside the normal routine or required a degree of specialized knowledge. These individuals completely planned and executed the placing of a plant in operation, developed and marketed a new product, instituted more effective financial controls, and carried out many other tasks. Each of these key men was a seasoned, broad-gauged individual, capable of assuming responsibility and getting the job done.

Since Kaiser knew people, and knew how to use them to maximum advantage, he realized that spot assignments were not the best technique to employ for an individual's long-term development. Therefore, on a planned basis, these men were gradually moved into line positions so that they could continue to function at a high motivational level. Once attuned to this modus operandi, they were able to rapidly shift gears and handle many varied jobs, or double in brass should an economic downturn occur.

At this time, for strategic and marketing reasons, the

company subdivided its efforts into two product groups—
valves and support equipment. Cryogenics,[12] a somewhat
unique product line, was spun off to become a completely
separate entity with a general manager responsible for sales,
engineering, manufacturing, and quality control.

In this realignment, Warren Kaiser assumed primary
responsibility for valve sales in order to give this major
segment of the business special attention and top executive
direction. One of his assistants was assigned the task of
backing his selling effort by handling the areas of sales administration, customer service, and estimating.

In addition, a second key individual was given the task of
establishing a more responsive cost accounting system and
dovetailing it into a project control system.

With an eye to the future, a new employee, Phil Letz, was
taken on to begin planning requirements for a new building.
We carefully checked Phil's qualifications at the time he was
hired to ensure that he was of sufficient calibre to be considered for the position of factory superintendent when the
new facility went on stream.

Thus, Phil not only did the planning and project activity,
but was actually being groomed to accept accountability for
the entire operation after the transition was completed.
Having Phil in complete charge of this new project permitted
those in manufacturing management to continue to concentrate on their day-to-day activities.

As the business continued to grow, the president smoothly
disengaged himself from primary responsibility for valve sales
and moved instead into the important policy areas of financial
planning, acquisitions, new product development, allocation
of resources, and management controls.

During this period Vortex Industries had strengthened its
product base with the most capable personnel in charge of
each product group. Once this horizontal base was secured,
the company began to expand each of these segments, with

---

[12] This company was developing valves for use in abnormally low temperature conditions and also processing liquids in a low-temperature range.

emphasis on product groups offering the greatest return on investment or long-term potential.

At this stage, the organizational structure was allowed to become more definitive with clearer lines of responsibility and accountability. For instance, engineering was separated into sections by major product group: military valves, commercial valves, support equipment, and cryogenics. These sections, in turn, were to be serviced by a centralized engineering services department.

With greater emphasis on product technology came a need for more exacting standards of quality. Therefore, the president decided to place quality control under his own wing, rather than with engineering or manufacturing.

To complement these changes, the director of finance was given the added responsibilities of contract administration and personnel relations. The plant manager retained basically the same duties as before—production, purchasing, materials management, and inspection.

The head of sales was made accountable for the complete sales function, including sales administration.

The key element in this approach to structuring an organization was to use people where they could do the most good at a particular point in the company's evolutionary development.

The results achieved by Vortex could be measured both in terms of accomplishments of specific missions and intermediate goals, and in its ability to advance people systematically into higher level positions such as factory superintendent, sales manager, manager of sales administration, budget director, and project control manager.

Moving steadily ahead, the company continued to grow through seeking out other areas of business opportunity. To accomplish this objective, Vortex developed individuals with skills in corporate planning and general management. These general assistants were expected to possess qualifications to replace or supplement talents of other key people, including the president.

Working in concert with members of management, these highly competent individuals became involved in market planning, organization planning, financial analysis, acquisitions and mergers, long- and short-range profit planning, product improvement and diversification, and other high priority assignments.

Throughout these years, there was never an overabundance of secretaries, clerks, or second level personnel. There were just a few key people who possessed the skills needed to enable Vortex to grow on a systematic and sound basis, and whose abilities were nurtured and developed by the company.

When a company draws little blocks on an organization chart, granted that it does identify specific areas of activity. But these blocks are too static to anticipate the influence that an individual's interests and capabilities may exert on his, and other, organizational components. Aggressiveness, self-motivation, and other personal traits defy accurate measurement. Although it may be possible to apportion responsibility among various members of management, it does not necessarily mean that results will follow accordingly. It is in the gray areas between organizational blocks where you separate the men from the boys—where initiative, drive, and results show up.

Let's look at functions within a typical business enterprise. As we said before, too often it's the same story: if you've seen one, you've seen them all. Basically, from one company to another, there is very little difference between purchasing, traffic, personnel, and general accounting. But there could be a decided difference in impact upon the organization if the scope and breadth of a function extended beyond the initiative-stifling constraints of those oblong blocks.

For instance, a traffic department maintains rates and tariffs, determines the least costly commodity classification to use, and plans the best route to ship its products. But what about logistics; warehousing; cost of inventories in transit; distribution; alternate shipping methods; unitized shipping containers; integrated transportation systems; and the use of methodology and techniques employed in operations research, linear programming, and computerization? The real payoff for traffic is in these areas, where the cream is waiting to be skimmed off. A company must encourage movement in these directions. Executive management cannot wait to be sold on "programs"; management must initiate the action.

A typical purchasing department goes through the ritual of contacting sources of supply; selecting the best vendor on the basis of price, delivery, quality, and service; and then placing an order. But when 40 to 60 percent of every sales dollar goes into outside purchased materials, a company has an obligation to look beyond this basic routine.

One company with which I worked closely in moving aggressively into these hallowed gray areas was Michigan Pneumatic. Bruce Wandell, the general purchasing agent, was a short, stocky, hard-bitten dynamo of a man. His primary interest was to expand and strengthen his support of the company in the vital areas of procurement and materials management.

To get started, Bruce and I held numerous sessions with people in engineering, manufacturing, and sales to determine exactly where and how parts and materials were used in the end product. The buyers were instructed by Wandell not to remain in the purchasing office but, instead, to go out where the action was—in the plant, with the engineer or draftsman, or working closely with a supplier. They soon *knew* what made their widget tick!

As a result, Wandell and his people were able to be more precise in their purchasing specifications and receive tighter competitive bids. Wandell constantly searched out ways to measure that hairline between minimum cost and acceptable performance. In most instances he found it. Not alone—but because he sought and obtained assistance from the company's cost accountants, industrial engineers, process engineers, and machine shop workers.

The purchasing function soon began to take on an activist identity that rippled throughout the organization.

Under Wandell's direction, the company only put into the

product purchased materials required to do the job. It avoided overspecifying. It cut down on size, gauge, tolerance, and other requirements that were not needed to produce a competitive product.

Wandell moved into quality considerations as well. He was instrumental in removing most subjective inspection decisions from purchased items. In one instance he got into a somewhat heated discussion with Darren Caldwell, the receiving inspector who was using the "thumbnail test" to check a burr on a pinion. The outcome of this difference of opinion was to accept that particular shipment but to develop more precise specifications for subsequent orders.

Eventually, Wandell mastered the function so completely that he was able to institute a value engineering program, engage in extensive contract purchasing, establish the technique of cost-benefit ratio analysis, and install a computerized vendor selection system.

Michigan Pneumatic now had the ability to control purchasing dollars and to reduce the cost of outside purchased parts and materials to an absolute minimum. During this period, purchases as a percentage of sales dropped 5 percent, rejections by 18 percent, and field complaints by 50 percent. The gray areas had taken on a dimension seldom seen before, and to Bruce Wandell this was only the beginning.

The U.S. federal government is a huge, massive structure. Its budget alone, in excess of $300 billion, exceeds the entire gross national product of any other country, with the exception of Russia and Japan. Within this colossus is a labyrinth of intricate webs that intertwine to form a network of bureaucratic departments, agencies, administrations, commissions, and other designations. Among this myriad of organizations is one that is a "little man," by federal standards, but has the economic clout of a "big man"—the Small Business Administration (SBA). Although dwarfed by cabinet-level giants such as the Departments of Defense, State, Commerce, and Health, Education and Welfare, in the final analysis the SBA may do more constructive good for more people than all the others combined.

The SBA is in itself big business, handling over $3 billion in direct or bank participation loans. SBA is involved in over thirty-five distinct areas of endeavor, from loans to individual small businesses, to subcontracting assistance and prime contract set-asides.

As stated a few years ago by the previous Deputy Administrator, Anthony Chase, "This agency has been a sleeping giant for eighteen years, but it's finally beginning to stir." And it's about time, because the SBA has the potential to solve every problem a small business might encounter.

It was about the time Tony Chase made this remark in a *Dun's Review* article on SBA that I was retained to aid in instituting an internal reorganization and revitalization program for the agency. My assignment was to establish a hard-hitting task force, composed of aggressive agency "doers," that would delve deeply into agency activities and report its findings to SBA management.

Tom Kleppe, the new administrator, was aware that soul-searching questions were being asked about SBA by the Office of Management and Budgets and by the Congress. He intended to find out how this vital agency could more effectively serve five million small businessmen who account for 37 percent of the gross national product. How could it streamline its internal procedures so that the 14,000 banks with which SBA does business could be assured that loan applications were being processed in the fastest, most expeditious manner? Also, how could SBA provide all the services it was designated to provide, at the least possible cost to the taxpayer?

To meet these demands the task force had to be results-oriented. As the task force leader and catalyst in this undertaking, my initial job was to carefully screen the agency people and select those who were qualified to serve on the task force. This meant finding highly motivated individuals with strong technical knowledge who would, above all, be willing to accept responsibility.

Each member of the group would have to understand that circumstances could develop in which his or her position might be in direct conflict with hard-core vested interests or with a strong opposing stance taken by a departmental superior. In these instances, the individual would be expected to accept the objectivity that this assignment entailed and be willing, if necessary, to "go to the mat" with someone in a higher executive post.

A task force serves a need when an organization is unable to move from its present position under normal management direction and requires greater concerted effort. By its very nature, a task force can have a tremendous impact on an organization. However, its built-in limitation is that those who are chosen from within to serve on the task force lack experience in a project of this magnitude; therefore, they must be willing to submerge their individuality within the framework of the total effort.

Once its members were selected, the task force immediately began to move aggressively toward fulfilling its mission. Each step was carefully defined. Ten specific objectives were to be accomplished. After these objectives were determined, a schedule of installation was prepared for use in planning and controlling the entire program. This schedule consisted of a series of detailed steps, in tightly controlled time frames, that would be used as the key planning device for the entire task force effort. It contained the actions required, the names of persons responsible, the time periods, the sequence of events, and the planned completion dates. The schedule indicated the expected movement of 350 tasks required to implement thirty projects involved in this program.

Projects were assigned priorities and the program was officially launched by Tom Kleppe at a kickoff meeting.

First on our list of projects was the establishment of an effective disaster loan program for presidentially declared national emergencies.

Within the previous six months, earthquakes had devastated the heart of Fairbanks, Alaska, and the suburban communities of Los Angeles. Floods had ravaged Pennsylvania and large sections of New England. Fires had cut a swath of death and destruction through the mountains of northern California. Damage to these areas was staggering, and SBA was responsible for providing emergency loans to the unfortunate victims of disasters which had been officially designated as national emergencies. Without question, this was the project with the highest priority. And it formed the pattern for all the others.

A task force team was assigned to the project, with one member who had expertise in financial assistance designated as the leader. A discussion was held to identify the objectives, scope, plan of action, critical milestone dates, and project completion date. Then the project team members were given these initial assignments:

1. Gather all available material on disaster loans.
2. Develop a preliminary table of contents as a guide to fact finding and assimilation of data.
3. Prepare a contingency plan checklist covering all disaster supply needs, personnel requirements, operating budgets, means of dissemination of public information, and legal requirements.

Within weeks, the project was completed and, upon approval by Tom Kleppe, was placed in operation.

A different combination of task force team members was soon enmeshed in projects dealing with SBA's 406 program involving grants and contracts to small business firms, SBA's internal executive reorganization, development of a means of allocating funds within the agency, loan credit evaluation and loan processing, the development of SBA policy formulation, and preparation of procedure manuals.

Four tough, back-breaking months went into this task force assignment. When the effort was completed, the agency was significantly stronger and better able to serve the needs of the business community. A complete management reform had been accomplished by the SBA in decentralizing authority, allocating responsibility and activities to the field, cutting through red tape, and streamlining the activity of federal assistance. All agency functions had been closely scrutinized and management improvements were made where problem areas existed.

A task force succeeds by concentrating a tremendous amount of talented manpower on solving a complex problem or on dealing with a set of extraordinary circumstances. The task force approach is used most productively for turn-arounds, profit improvement programs, management information systems, operations research, and strategic business planning.

E. K. Wood, Inc. developed an effective method of operating its enterprise. Franklin Wood, board chairman, was a New Englander who told me, "Profits come from people. People use machines, materials, and systems—not the other way around. People, from the hourly laborer to the chairman of the board, all contribute to a company's success."

During our first encounter, Wood continued to explain his philosophy of management to me. He stated, "People must 'grow' in their jobs. E. K. Wood did this by increasing their incentive, both in the paycheck and through pride of accomplishment. We must know who the achievers are—and get them into the action spots fast—and weed them out from the others. Also, we must be willing to pitch in when these men are in trouble because, at one time or another, even the very best people encounter their reverses."

My assignment was to work with Franklin Wood and his people in developing different techniques to optimize the organization's impact. Project teams and task forces were placed in motion to accomplish major objectives. We opted against going the committee route by having only one person in charge of any given task.

It soon became evident that this method nurtured talent faster than conventional line and staff organizational approaches by accelerating the management development process. A formal "skills inventory" data bank was used to locate and rapidly assign people with the needed capabilities to a project or job. By providing people with greater opportunity to express their individual initiative, the company was able to live up to its recruiting promise that working at E. K. Wood would be a stimulating experience.

Over the coming years, there probably will be more firms using the E. K. Wood approach or possibly even a more drastic method referred to as "temporary management systems." Under this concept, people who have skills to contribute to the solution of a particular problem meet for a short time, make their contribution, and then depart. Perhaps they never become members of any fixed and permanent management group.

Top management's role will be to oversee the totality of the enterprise and try to identify the strategic moves to be made in a changing and growing business environment. As new approaches are developed by the incumbent executive management, it must seek and acquire the desired combinations of talent which will enable the company to move aggressively into areas of growth opportunity.

This technique may make it possible for a company to remain trim and hard even while expanding, so that should a slackening in the economy develop, it will have a minimal effect upon the enterprise.

The metabolism of the corporate body does not react favorably to the temporary expedient of crash reducing diets or pep pills. Instead, the company must be constantly nourished with fresh ideas and imaginative innovations if it is to remain vigorous. Otherwise, it will sink into despair at the first unfavorable shiftings in the business climate and slowly drift into oblivion.

12
The Management
Consultant's
Smorgasbord

This chapter is a smorgasbord of consulting assignments that covered a wide range of typical business problems. Each assignment had its own particular mixture of unusual and complex conditions. Many occurred in companies with historical significance that enhanced the fabric and texture of the encounter.

The Petrillo Construction Company originated during the arms build-up in the early years of World War I. Nicholas Petrillo began the business by collecting scrap metal for the war effort in a rickety old pushcart. He worked along the southwest edges of Brooklyn and in the Park Slope section of that borough. When he had collected a load, he would wheel his cart across the Brooklyn Bridge to Manhattan, where he would sell the metal at the current scrap value for conversion into cast iron cannons, howitzer shells, or bullets for an infantryman's rifle.

Over the following three decades, the company had evolved into a carpentry subcontractor. Then, when Nicholas's sons, Vincent and Silvio, had mastered the building trade, the firm became a general contractor. Now, in the early 1970s, Petrillo Construction had sales of $15 million, mostly in state and municipal contracts for the construction of hospitals, psychiatric centers, and prisons in New York and New Jersey.

Cash flow had been great for a number of years, since it is possible in the building industry to front load a job by estimating the percentage of completion on the high side in the early stages, receiving a big advance payment from the holder of the builder's loan, and using this cash to plow back into additional projects.

Since the construction industry normally has low profits (2 to 3 percent) but high return on invested capital (20 to 30 percent), front-end money gives the builder tremendous leverage in expanding the operation. Unfortunately, if the company isn't tightly controlled, the day of reckoning eventually comes when the earlier jobs have long and costly "punch lists" of unfinished work and insufficient funds to wrap them up. Then the general contractor may be in default of his contract, forfeit the retainer, and often be forced into bankruptcy. Petrillo Construction had fallen victim to this practice by overextending itself and was in an extremely precarious financial position.

Vincent Petrillo, the president of the firm and Nicholas's eldest son, contacted me through the firm's attorney and asked for my assistance. After investigating the situation, I met with Vincent and indicated that the company sorely needed an effective cost accounting system, tight budgetary controls, and responsive financial reports if it was to stay alive. Petrillo Construction was guilty of a cardinal sin that is commonplace in the business world—it didn't know the costs of running the business profitably.

Installing a cost accounting system is laborious, detailed work. There are no shortcuts. With Petrillo Construction, as with other companies, determining material costs (other than subcontract work) required an analysis of all vendor invoices, and then a judgment decision on how much inflation would affect prices during the coming accounting period. Some firms adjust costs continually as significant price changes occur and use new cost schedules for estimating purposes, while others only change cost figures yearly (or less frequently).

Petrillo did many jobs with company labor so it also needed accurate labor costs. Project managers had to account for all field laborers' work and then check these hours against those shown on time cards. Indirect labor, selling, and administrative costs were also required to reflect proper charges to specific jobs.

Working closely with Sal DeNinno, the head of accounting, I developed a chart of accounts to classify each item going into the balance sheet or into the profit and loss statement.

Previously, subcontractor transactions had been posted to individual ledger sheets with jobs commingled. Burning the midnight oil, Sal and I laboriously transferred subcontractor transactions from this outdated method to a dual system with controls established by subcontractor and project. In addition, the new system had the capability to automatically post transactions on an electronic bookkeeping machine.

Accurate cost figures were now available for estimating purposes. No more shooting crap and taking a beating on the job before one brick was laid. Bids could now be made on a selective basis according to what the Petrillo Construction Company could do best. That's what a good cost system should—and must—do.

Budgets were the next task to be tackled. The company had none. Vincent Petrillo would compare a new job with a previous one, and then determine on that rule-of-thumb basis how long the new job would take and about what it would cost.

A budgetary control system was designed to compare actual expenditures against budget. However, the mere installation of a budgetary control system would be inadequate if the means to stay within budget wasn't established as well.

Detailed project schedules were plotted by the critical path method[13] and the data were computerized. The company was

---

[13] The critical path method was developed by the U.S. Navy. It is used to establish all the components of a project and isolating or pinpointing, through predetermined time elements, which are the essential activities that must remain within schedule.

about to begin a $3 million building complex at the Lindale psychiatric hospital in northern New Jersey. Under "normal" circumstances, the completion of this project would have taken Petrillo Construction four years and would have shown a loss; using critical path, it was possible to plan the job for three years at an expected profit of 4 percent.

The control of time is dependent on a tight, realistic schedule. This is cost control through adherence to budgets.

On the Lindale project, a detailed schedule was prepared, with each job component broken down so that no step would exceed twenty working days. The information was then keypunched and placed on a computer. If a significant delay should occur during the life of the project, such as a sub-contractor default, the schedule would be automatically redone and, if necessary, the budget adjusted accordingly. However, every effort would be made to defray all, or a major portion, of the expected overrun through changes in schedule that would compensate for the delay.

The detailed project schedule for Lindale was developed by the field superintendent and Silvio Petrillo who was general superintendent, before final review and approval by the president, Vincent Petrillo. Once they were established, the job data were constantly maintained and updated by a top-level home office coordinator.

After the schedule was developed, the estimating section worked with the accounting department to develop a budget for each item of expense. Each item was coded by reference to a newly developed cost control code book. The budget consisted of a total amount for each item as well as month-by-month figures. Overhead was allocated to the job and was shown both in total and as a monthly running expense.

At the end of each month, two financial control reports were prepared for management: a monthly project report and a report showing budget versus actual costs. The general superintendent was required to explain variances from budget (plus or minus 5 percent) and to see that action was taken to get back on budget.

A financial report was developed to furnish management

with a periodic summary of all significant data for each active project. It covered contract amount, amount requisitioned to date, less amount retained (usually ten percent), net amount received, cost to date, receipts less costs, balance remaining on contract, less balance due subcontractors, less amount to complete project, less allocated overhead, net profit (or loss) less amount retained, retainage due (amount still due contractor), net profit (or loss) on project, and net profit.

From these data an accurate monthly profit and loss statement was prepared. The report also showed critical financial facts such as cash flow, amount due subcontractors, amount to be spent to complete each project, and amount in retainage.

Each month the financial analysis report, budget report, and subcontractors' report were analyzed by Sal DeNinno, and a cover letter was prepared for Vincent and Silvio Petrillo, highlighting the significant figures in the reports.

In addition to the Lindale job, the company had twelve other active projects. It took us over a year to get a firm grip on the business. This is usually the case in industries engaged in long lead-time projects.

Petrillo Construction also had to purge itself of the effects of many years of financial neglect. But the controls worked. Today the company is on a sound operating basis, bidding on state and municipal jobs, and also building two-family housing units and renovating old office buildings. These latter two growth areas were a dividend spotted by the "robot" cost accounting system which presumably was taught only to spit out vital statistics—not to think.

The Curtiss-Wright Corporation has one of the most exciting corporate histories of any company in existence. On December 17, 1903, Wilbur and Orville Wright made the world's first flight in a power driven, heavier-than-air machine at Kitty Hawk, North Carolina. Orville Wright piloted the plane, having won the privilege by the toss of a coin. He flew 120 feet and remained in the air for twelve seconds. Today, the old reliable Lockheed C-5A transport workhorse has a wingspread greater than 120 feet.

The Wrights continued their flying experiments at a field near Dayton, Ohio, in 1904 and 1905. In 1904, they made 105 flights but totaled only forty-five minutes in the air, although two flights lasted five minutes each. On October 5, 1905, their machine flew 24.2 miles in thirty-eight minutes and three seconds.

On the morning of September 9, 1908, Orville made fifty-seven complete circles over the drill field at Fort Myer, Virginia, at an altitude of 120 feet. He remained in the air for one hour and two minutes and established several records on the same day.

In August, 1909, the Wrights closed a contract with some wealthy men in Germany for the formation of a German Wright Company. Later in the year, they formed the Wright Company in New York City to manufacture airplanes.

From this less than auspicious beginning, the Curtiss-Wright Corporation was formed. In 1918 the company built the Curtiss Jenny for use by U.S. Army pilots flying the first continuously scheduled airmail service. A Curtiss NC-4 preceded Lindbergh to Paris with a transatlantic flight in May, 1919. Lindbergh's flight in 1927 was made with a Wright engine.

By World War II, the aviation industry had grown to be one of the largest in the U.S. Curtiss-Wright had changed from an aircraft manufacturer to become the leading producer of airplane engines. At its peak, Curtiss-Wright was the second largest industrial company in the United States, exceeded in sales volume only by the automotive giant, General Motors.

In 1942, the United States produced 47,000 planes (more than all the planes manufactured in the thirty-seven years after the Wright Brothers' first flight). In 1944, the figure soared to 96,000. In all, more than 300,000 planes were produced in the years from 1940 to 1945, with Curtiss-Wright the main supplier of the power plants.

After World War II, aircraft designers made swift progress

in the development of jet-propelled planes. Then came turbo-jets and turboprops, the former with the advantage of higher speeds and the latter with greater fuel economy.

Soon the aerospace industry became involved in the complexities of supersonic, rocket-powered aircraft. More powerful planes were required to withstand tremendously high speeds and the temperature extremes encountered in flying through the "heat barrier."

This frenetic period demanded the utmost in aerospace technology from those in the field. The competition was so severe that many leading companies were unable to maintain their position in the industry. Curtiss-Wright was one of these firms. By the mid-1960s, Curtiss-Wright was no longer a primary manufacturer of airplane engines.

However, to remain in the engine business, it had obtained exclusive North American patent rights to a rotating combustion engine called the Wankel engine, after its inventor, Felix Wankel. After making many refinements in the engine and completing 35,000 hours of intensive testing, Curtiss-Wright was in a position to display the rotating combustion (RC) engine to prospective customers. This engine had some basic advantages over other conventional engines used for light aircraft, marine craft, automobiles, snowmobiles, and similar vehicles. These advantages were:

- More HP per pound of engine than a piston engine.
- Fewer total moving parts.
- No reciprocating parts—minimal vibrations.
- Acceptance of fuels of various octane ratings.
- Supplied torque for about two-thirds of the combustion cycle, compared to one-fourth for piston engines.

Thus, Curtiss-Wright was in a position to move aggressively into three segments of the rapidly expanding leisure-time industry (air, marine, and winter sports), as well as into basic vehicular transportation.

I met with Julian Hendricks, corporate marketing vice-president, to discuss the assignment. Hendricks quickly stated the purpose of our meeting. "Jerry, I want you to make a detailed study and document all of the factors involved in the RC engine program. Also, lay out a blueprint for Curtiss-Wright on how it can produce and market the Wankel engine profitably."

Since Hendricks wanted to activate this program after it had been so many years in the incubation stage, he ended the conversation by offering to provide me with strong in-house support. "I will provide you with a team of about twenty design engineers, cost accountants, industrial engineers, manufacturing people, facilities and machine tool specialists, and members of the marketing staff, to aid in the project. If you need additional assistance, it will be given to you. Best of luck!"

It was now my job to develop a strategic business plan that would get Curtiss-Wright back into the manufacture of engines—where it rightfully belonged—through a technological advancement in the state of the art that could give the company a dominant marketing position well into the next decade.

When I met with the twenty team members in the corporate conference room, our first order of business was to develop the specific objectives of the assignment. We had to determine the type of organizational structure required to produce the RC engine; a method of making it a self-sustaining investment center; the manpower requirements at various levels of sales activity; the plant facilities and equipment requirements; the automated production capability and manufacturing work flow; a method of controlling production and inventories, field service support, and projected sales growth; import and licensing requirements; quotas for "set aside" spare engine replacement needs; and the method for activating the program.

Field trips were made to primary market areas to gather firsthand knowledge on how purchasing agents would accept the "Wankel" engine and the approximate number of units that could be sold.

Other team members moved ahead with judgments in the

areas of engineering, manufacturing, and accounting. From this activity, it was decided to hold overhead costs down by drawing heavily from the parent organization.

The strategic business plan contained a summary of financial data indicating when the "Wankel" engine would achieve a break-even point and Curtiss-Wright could expect to recover its investment.

After all the work was completed on the project, it was presented to Julian Hendricks and other members of executive management for consideration. Curtiss-Wright now had a documented program upon which to reenter the highly competitive engine market with a product that was patent protected. They could now move aggressively into various segments of the market that offered the greatest long-term growth potential.

In fact, the RC engine, with its simple design and few moving parts, would have been the perfect engine for two gentlemen named Wilbur and Orville Wright to use when testing a new-fangled contraption on a chilly December morn at a place called Kitty Hawk, back in the year 1903.

Matthias William Baldwin pioneered the use of steam for locomotives, following in the footsteps of the Scottish inventor, James Watt, who had patented a working model of a steam engine in 1769. In 1832, Baldwin advertised in a Philadelphia paper that a locomotive engine known as Old Ironsides would depart daily, when the weather was fair, with a train of passenger cars. On rainy days, horses would be attached. The engine had a speed of twenty-eight miles an hour and pulled thirty tons. Quite an achievement in those days.

In 1854, the Baldwin Locomotive Works was formed. By the time of Baldwin's death in 1866, the company had turned out more than fifteen hundred locomotives. Development of better, more functional, models continued through the years until steam locomotives had carved a permanent niche for themselves in the annals of American history.

During its peak production period from 1920 to 1930, the Baldwin Locomotive Company was efficiently producing thirty engines per month in a mile-long manufacturing facility. Beside this enormous building stood a roundhouse for testing completed engines, a machine shop for making engine parts, and a foundry capable of casting axles, shafts, wheels, and other vital engine components.

In the early 1930s General Motors, the automotive giant, developed a diesel engine and began to compete with Baldwin in a newly formed entity known as the Electro-Motive Division. The division had many technical problems to iron out in the manufacture of diesels; and as the thirties rolled on, proud Baldwin Locomotive disregarded the upstart and pushed ahead full throttle with improved versions of steam locomotives.

Then World War II erupted and soon the United States was involved. The government needed locomotive engines desperately to keep materials moving to and from the war production plants. Contracts were awarded to Baldwin to build steam locomotives and to Electro-Motive to produce diesels. Both companies were "frozen" into the engine type they were most skilled at making. Then the war ended and customers wanted diesel engines only. The curtain had rung down on the glamorous age of Matthias William Baldwin's steam locomotive.

Ten years later, only a shell of the company remained. Baldwin Locomotive merged with a midwestern machinery manufacturer and was renamed the Baldwin-Lima-Hamilton Company. A few steam engines still were produced for Argentina, Brazil, and other South American and Asian countries, but volume orders were nonexistent. Spare parts were still being ordered to keep older engines in the field in operation, but even this business was drying up fast. Machine tools were mostly prewar vintage and even skilled machinists had difficulty maintaining tolerances. The foundry had lost most of its captive business and was forced to compete with smaller, more responsive foundries for additional work. Job shop production demanded fast deliveries of castings—unlike the good old days when the steam locomotive plant would order well in advance with a three-month schedule of requirements.

As a result, drastic action was needed by Baldwin-Lima-Hamilton to salvage what it could from the existing foundry operation.

Working closely with the new general manager, Alfred Kroll, a weather-beaten veteran of thirty years in the trade, I recognized that strong and positive measures were needed. Within weeks, a sales manager was hired to develop a sales force powerful enough to market the foundry's capabilities against competition from the independents.

A financial critique of B-L-H operations compared with similar foundries indicated that the return on investment was so low that unless profits could be materially increased, the division would have to shut down. An investigation revealed the reasons for the poor profits—customers were dissatisfied with the foundry because of late delivery and poor quality.

Steps were taken immediately to develop a sound production control system that would provide reliable, on-time delivery. All basic elements in the production cycle were flowcharted in detail. The cycle began with the receipt of a sales order from the sales department that was often an extremely long-winded document containing too much information. In one instance, a sales order contained the entire Code of the City of New York on twenty-four single-spaced pages. Every word was laboriously retyped on a twelve-part foundry production order. Almost one thousand orders were prepared in this manner each month, with copies forwarded to various internal departments and fabricating shops.

Move tickets were prepared to identify the pattern and core box when it was ready to be moved from the pattern shop to the foundry. A pattern transfer list was also prepared to move patterns in and out of storage. Then there were more forms, such as a pattern shop schedule, a defective casting report, a record of cylinder liners, a casting cleaning list, a delivered foundry output report, an open order report, a foundry tonnage shipped report, an intershop request for delivery dates on productive materials, and a daily charge report.

Altogether, the existing production control system used twenty-three different reports and forms. No wonder deliveries were slow—the casting took three days to make while the paperwork took three weeks.

A new system was designed that combined all information on one foundry production order consisting of a deck of twelve operation cards and a master control card. Data captured on each card included estimated weight of each casting, material specification number, product class, quantity required, molding bed number, furnace or ladle number, and scheduled start and completion dates for molding and pouring.

In addition, the cards contained the sales order number, part number, part name, pattern number, pattern instruction, general remarks, and a place for an inspection stamp.

The reverse side of the operation cards was used as a time card with quantity, price, and earnings amount posted in part by the foundry worker and then automatically extended by computer.

A computer printout gave the foundry its load factor. Weekly schedules were run on the computer and then "fine" scheduled in the foundry office on visual schedule control boards to provide greater flexibility.

Foundry scheduling was done in two steps: the first time element covered pattern and core box making, and the second phase covered all production operations. As a job moved through each production step in the cycle—coremaking, molding, pouring, cleaning, and chipping—a prepunched card would be returned as evidence of completed work. Each of the twenty-four molding beds was loaded daily and adjusted if changes in plan occurred. The same applied to the pouring schedule for controlling work going into each furnace and ladle.

Every step in the production cycle was tightly controlled.

Paperwork delays were eliminated. Orders were shipped on time—within days—with replacement castings expedited through the foundry. Rejections were sharply reduced and quality was maintained according to customer specifications.

Savings in overhead costs and direct labor gave the foundry leverage in maintaining prices at competitive levels.

Perhaps castings aren't as glamorous as locomotives. But customer needs change over the years and companies must adjust to prevailing circumstances in order to survive.

The foundry helped to stabilize B-L-H operations. Once the erosion of its resources had been stopped, the division was able to forge ahead into the mainstream of acceptable profitability with a well-balanced product mix.

It began to concentrate on products such as turbines to generate power for hydroelectric plants, testing machines to check quality reliability, strain gauges to control production through use of sensor devices, and preform presses and hydraulic presses to aid in the manufacture of large intricate shapes.

In his lifetime, Matthias William Baldwin would never have borne witness to the products now being produced by B-L-H. But then, none of these could ever hope to match the excitement that was generated the first time Old Ironsides rode through town.

Every schoolboy can recite the details of Paul Revere's midnight ride through the countryside around Lexington, Massachusetts, warning the people that the British were coming. But few would know that Paul was one of the most highly skilled metal artisans of his time. He was a caster of cannons and bells, a silversmith, a shipfitter, and a craftsman who sheathed the roof of the Massachusetts statehouse and the hull of the *Constitution* with copper. The emphasis placed on his equestrian episode has obscured his true stature as a pioneer manufacturer and industrialist. Paul Revere set down strong roots for what is today the Revere Copper and Brass Company, a $400 million metalworking firm.

Adamson Extrusions, located in Bensenville, Illinois, thirty miles north of the windy city of Chicago, had sales of about $8 million a year. Certainly not much compared to the giant Revere Copper and Brass. But there was one mutual bond between the two firms—Revere supplied Adamson with aluminum billets, rods, tubes, and other materials used to make aluminum extrusions, finished aluminum window frames, and other exterior products.

However, Adamson was unable to make payment for a substantial amount of material recently purchased from Revere, because it was suffering from a case of indigestion due to a recent acquisition. Although potentially sound, Adamson Extrusions now badly needed assistance to integrate the new acquisition and to improve plant operations if it was to remain in business and meet its creditor obligations.

Revere Copper and Brass, as its primary supplier, was aware of Adamson's precarious position and offered its assistance. This was a most unusual gesture, rarely found in the world of business. I personally know of only one other instance when a supplier acted to aid a customer in a critical situation, although there may have been many such cases.

Years ago, Joseph Connelly had been virtually wiped out in a fire that destroyed the Connelly Container Corporation in Conshohocken, Pennsylvania, on the outskirts of Philadelphia. Suppliers helped put Connelly back in business. As a result, he was able to salvage his enterprise and, within a few years, he became chief executive officer of the Crown Cork and Seal Company where his impressive turnaround made him a living legend in business circles.

I was engaged to assist Adamson Extrusion by Bob Altenburger, an administrative executive in the home office of Revere Copper and Brass. He explained the problem in general terms, indicating that the objective of the task was to get the company back on a sound financial basis.

The following morning I boarded the 7:00 A.M. businessman's flight to Chicago, where I was met by Ward Adamson, president of the company. An hour later we were in

207

his office overlooking the plant, ready to begin work. Adamson had built the business from scratch, so he was willing to accept any outside help that could salvage the company. After a few hours of heavy discussion sandwiched around a plant tour, we were ready to begin the program.

First, a break-even chart was prepared to determine at which point the company could start to make a profit. Then, specific responsibilities for each key person were clearly defined. Next, a detailed action plan was developed with a timetable to accomplish 102 improvements in the plant—with the entire plan programmed for completion within three months.

We began the program the following morning and constructive improvements came fast and furiously—machine loading; shop order control; job instruction training of factory workers; job tickets controlled through time clock punching; downtime code control; procedure for timekeeping activity; training of timekeepers; analyzing job cost variances; job cost reporting system; learning curve for inexperienced and newly employed operators in fabrication, buffing, anodizing, and packing.

Ward Adamson and his people were really barrelling along on all eight cylinders. Moving into high gear, we soon put in downtime reporting and control, procedure for purchasing of tooling on new orders, procedure for handling reorders, procedure for handling sample orders, plan to reduce small order volume, analysis of marginal business, ready reference table for bidding purposes, and a review procedure of customers' orders where extra operations may be eliminated.

We even communicated to the salesmen what was being done in the factory to make their job easier. Then we followed up with a realistic sales incentive plan to increase volume. And as frosting for the cake, we prepared a plant capability brochure containing all technical information needed by sales to promote additional business.

Other changes we made included a review of process sheets for completeness and correct sequencing of operations;

development of a method to coordinate engineering, sales and manufacturing; establishment of time elements for processing orders; development of purchasing procedure to insure material availability when required by manufacturing; and development of a policy statement defining sales responsibility for the sale of excess material.

Two months had gone by and the changes were beginning to pay off. However, we still had other tasks to complete, such as developing a method for coordinating tooling for manufacturing needs, establishing a policy on samples, and developing lead time schedules for sales.

In addition, we determined the location for excess material, established hold areas, and marked and identified aisles and obstructions.

Our time schedule was being met and we had accomplished the improvements as planned. There were now only a few tasks remaining—developing applications where the mill could supply all material ready for processing in the trim shop; implementing a materials handling program and tool maintenance program; changing the layout in inspection and packing; and determining hydraulic cart specifications.

Also, we developed methods improvements on rework of saws, bulk acid storage, the buffing area, the tool crib, three-color tank, unipunch setup, multiple drill press, and automatic cutoff.

Finally, the project was completed with the preparation of an analytical profile of profitable accounts for management's use, development of a six-month profit path control chart, development of management reports to compare actual costs against standard costs, and the establishment of financial control reports to audit future operating performance.

Adamson Extrusions had gone through its baptism of fire and grown in stature. The company had been saved from the brink of disaster. But this time, through foresight, the descendants of Paul Revere had averted a calamitous event without a midnight ride and shouts of "one if by land and two if by sea."

Index

Acme Wire Company, 3-4
"Act of God" changes, 26-27
Ad agency, use of, 16
Adams, Nelson, 98, 99
Adamson, Ward, 207-208
Adamson Extrusions, 207-209
Advanced Packaging Technology,
    promotion package for, 49-53
Advertising industry, 70, 71
Altenburger, Bob, 207
Ambrose, Austin, 178-180
Ametal, Ltd., 147
Arkwright, Sir Richard, 1
Ashland Oil Company, 70
Assignments, obtaining, 15-19
Association of Consulting Management
    Engineers (ACME), 6
Association of Management Con-
    sultants (AMC), 6
Automated equipment, idea for (new
    business venture), 53-56

Babbage, Charles, 1
Baldwin, Matthias William, 202, 206
Baldwin Locomotive Works, 202-203
Baldwin-Lima-Hamilton Company,
    202-206
Bankruptcy, 57, 59
Barton's (credit appliance chain), 64-65

Bee, Mary, 144
Bell, Alexander Graham, 53
Benton, Jack, 102
Bethlehem Steel Corporation, 36
Bible Prayer and Joint Worship
    Institute, profit improvement
    program, 124-127
Bixby, Hilton, 131-133
Bjork, Eivind, 122
Blazer, Rexford S., 70
Boating industry, salesmanship in, 71-
    77
Booz, Ed, 5
Boulton, Matthew Robinson, 1
Brach, Philip, 143, 146
Brill, Roger, 89-91
Browning, Frank, 28

Caldwell, Darren, 188
Carburetion device, idea for (new
    business venture), 41-45
Carlson, Doug, 72
Carnegie, Andrew, 35-36
Ceco Industries Company, 18
Certain-teed Products Company, 18
Charter Rent-A-Car, turnaround
    program, 105-109
Chase, Anthony, 189
Clark, Vincent, 111

Index

Client referrals, 15
Cocktail party, salesmanship by, 75
Collective bargaining, 10
Companies:
  evolutionary pattern of, 37
  pilferage, theft, and misappropriation
    of funds in, 57–67
  turnarounds, 89–109
  See also New business ventures
Computer Supplies Corporation (CSC),
    84–85, 86
Computer systems, 128–149, 162–163
  applications to business (case
    histories), 133–149
  international copper trading, 146–
    149
  in manufacturing, 134–138
  MRP system, 138–140
  in publishing 140–146
  during 1950s, 129
  growth of (1960–1970s), 136–137
  histograms, 134
  medium-scale, 137
  mini-, 137
  operations research methodology,
    133–134, 135
  specialization, 129–130
Connaughton, James, 159
Connelly, Joseph, 207
Connelly Container Corporation, 207
Consolidated Petroleum, profit
    planning program, 169–171
Consulting assignments, range and
    types of, 194–209
Corporate personality, evaluation of, 29
Cosmetics industry, sales promotion
    techniques, 71
Credit stores, 77–80
Crest Manufacturing Company, 18
Crown Cork and Seal Company, 207
Curtain Corporation of America, 10–12
Curtiss-Wright Corporation, 198–202

Data processing, *see* Computer systems
Demonstration, salesmanship by, 75
DeNinno, Sal, 196
Denning, Leonard, 126
Denville Rubber Company, turnaround
    program, 89–98
  basis of reorganization, 91

budget and financial reports, 93–94
employee participation, 92–93
MTM standards, 93
operating divisions formed from, 91–
    92
profit margins, 97–98
sales policy, 95–96, 97
strengthening the product line, 94–95
training program, 96
Diamond, Bob, 47–48
Discount book promoters, 82
Discounting, sales by, 82–84
Du Pont Corporation, 53, 151
Dun and Bradstreet, 13
Dun's Review, 189
Durant, William C., 36
Dyna-Craft Yacht Company, 58–59

E. K. Wood, Inc., 192–193
Edison, Thomas, 53
Egerson, Howard, 122
8A program, 85–86
Eisenhower, Dwight D., 152
Electronics Division, 131–133
Engel, Allen, 26–27
Engel, Werner, 26–27
Evershevski, Ted, 143
Executive management, 150–163
  associates selected by, 152–153
  economy and, 181–193
    business cycle, 181–182
    strategic planning, 183–193
  organizational planning, 152
  primary requisite of, 151–152
  Red Dog game applied to, 153–158
  subordinates and, 151, 163
  success factors, 150–151
  unfortunate type of, 151
Executive Sales Program (ESP), 75

Family-operated business, 20–26
  accepting recommended changes in,
    24–25
  mother's interference, 21–22
  relationship conflicts in, 22–23
Farnsworth, Tom, 44
Farrington Steel Company, 28–29
Fisherman's Wharf idea (new business
    venture), 38–41
Flight simulators, programming of, 130

Follow-up, salesmanship by, 75
Folsom, Hank, 27–28
Forbes Paint Company, 112
Ford, Henry, 2, 140
Ford Motor Company, 2
Fortune, 13
FPC Company, 27–28
Friendly Bargain Stores, profit improvement program, 114–120
outline for, 117–120
sales volume from, 120
strategy for, 116–117
Front-office study, 25–26
Frost, Hugh, 143
Fry, George, 5

Gantt, Harry, 2
Garvey, Chester, 41–45
Garvey, Mrs. Chester, 44
Garvey, J. Walter, 164–169
Gasoline exhaust fumes, idea for control of, 41–45
Geneen, Harold, 155
General Electric Company, 53
General Motors Corporation, 36, 203
General Service Administration (GSA), 85
Gilbreth, Frank, 2
Gillette, King, 36
Glamorene Company, 18
Gordon, Gene, 105–109
Granatelli, Andy, 70
Graphic Sports News and Views, 140–146
Gross national product, 188
Group meeting, salesmanship by, 75
Guest speaker appearances, 15

Hamilton, Carl, 5
Harmon, Brad, 95
Harper, Tom, 29
Harvey Test Products, 138–140
Hendricks, Julian, 200–201
"Hip pocket" accounts, 15
Hudson River Day Liners, 38

Industrial engineering, beginning of, 2
Industrial Revolution, 1
Industry, major functions of, 153–154
Industry seminars, participation at, 15

Institute of Management Consultants (IMC), 6
International Business Machines Corporation (IBM), 53, 151
IBM 360/30 Model, 136
IBM 360/40 Model, 114
IBM 370/Model 35, 136
IBM 370/Model 115, 136
IBM 402, 403, 407 Models, 129
IBM 602A Model, 129
IBM 604 Model, 129
IBM 1401 Model, 136
IBM 6400 machines, 30–31, 32, 33
Inventories, recommendations for (to prevent loss in jewelry business), 60–61, 62, 63

Jameson, Steven, 84–85, 86
Johnson, Lyndon, 152
Jones, Henry, 53–56
Junior executives, 151, 163

Kaiser, Warren, 183–186
Keating, Ken, 97
Kennedy, John F., 152
KF Industries, profit planning program, 177–180
Klechinski, Jenina, 23
Klechinski, Peter, 23–25
Klechinski, Tom, 24
Kleppe, Tom, 189, 190, 191
Knight, Paul, 112
Kroll, Alfred, 204

Larceny, in industry, 63–67
Laundry business, family owned, 23–25
Lehman, Nathan, 115–116
Let Us All Pray and Worship Together, 124
Letz, Phil, 184
Lie detector tests, use of, 67
Life, 140
Lindbergh, Charles, 199
Little, Roy 155
London Metal Exchange, 146–149
London Metals Company, 147, 149
Lonegan, Joe, 146
Long Island Lighting Company, 24
Look, 140
Lundberg, Martin, 125, 126–127

Index

Mail order catalog business, 36
Mail solicitation, 15
Management consultants:
  academic qualifications for, 13
  advisory role of, 9–10
  associations for, 6
  cost of, 9, 12, 15
  expertise of, 5–6, 13
  fields of competence, 5–6
  growth of, 1–7
  independent, 14–15
  large firm, 14
  management services (of major ac-
    counting firm), 14
  medium-sized (small specialty shop),
    14
  mid-1940s type of, 5, 6
  program applications, 6
  regional speciality house, 14
  research-oriented, 14
  types of, 14–15
Material requirements planning (MRP),
  103, 138
Mavericks, corporate, 27–28, 29
Methods-time-motion (MTM) standards, 93
Michigan Pneumatic Company, 187–
  188
Mid-Town Jewelers, 77–80
Midvale Steel Company, 1–2
Minority companies, 85–86
Misappropriation of company funds,
  57–67
  case histories, 58–67
    larceny, 63–67
    pilferage, 57–63
Model T Fords, 2
Modern Carpet Sweeper Company, 18
Monte Carlo, gambling casino at, 113
Moody's, 13
Morgan, J. P., 36
Morton, Lou, 47

Nadine Company, 87, 88
New business ventures, 35–56
  case histories, 38–56
  entrepreneur (nineteenth century), 35-
    -36
  methods of financing, 37–38
  role of consultant in, 38

New York Boat Show, 120, 123
New York Times, The, 149
Newark race riots, 80
Nixon, Richard, 152–153
Northeast Paint and Varnish Company,
    profit improvement program,
    110–114
  project control system, 111–112
  savings impact from, 112–114

Occupational Safety and Health Act, 6
Ocean Breeze Yacht Company, 71–77
  steps in sales planning process for, 74-
    -75
Office of Management and Budgets, 189
Omnitech Industries, 54–55
Operations research, 192

Parker Pulp and Paper, 159–162
Paternalism, 29
Pennsylvania Railroad Company, 35
Personality quirks, partnership and, 29–
  33
Peterson, Jon, 92
Petrillo, Nicholas, 194, 197
Petrillo, Silvio, 194, 197
Petrillo, Vincent, 194, 195, 196
Petrillo Construction Company, 194–
  197
Pilferage, control of, 57–63
Playtime Togs, 64
Preplanning, salesmanship by, 75
Private detective agencies, using, 65–67
Production control systems, types of, 11
Profit improvement program, 110–127,
  192
  purpose of, 110
Profit planning, 164–180
  compared to organization planning,
    177
  planning and control, 177–180

Qualified prospects, salesmanship by,
  75

Radio Corporation of America (RCA),
  53
Rainette (manufacturers), 25–26
Reardon, Mario, 105–109
Red Dog (gambling game), 153–158

Reinhardt, Raymond, 167, 168
Repeat business, 15
Revere, Paul, 206, 209
Revere Copper and Brass Company, 18, 206, 207

Salesmanship, 68–88
  Arabian Nights story, 68
  best anecdote on, 69
  in boating industry, 71–77
  case histories, 71–88
  minority group participation, 84–86
  and planning long-range growth, 86–88
  in retail store, 77–84
Saturday Evening Post, 140
Schmidt, Lars, 123
Schwab, Charles M., 36
Schwartz, Ruben, 77–84
Sears and Roebuck, 36
Second generation sons, business torment and degradation of, 33–34
Security chiefs, using (to control pilferage), 63
Serialized move ticket system, 58
Service industries, 48–49
Sew-Rite Company, 87, 88
Silvers, Stanley, 172–177
Simulated "dollar" bills, sales by, 81–82
Slimfit label, profit planning program, 171–177
Small Business Administration (SBA), 37, 84, 188–192
  loans handled by, 189
Society of Professional Management Consultants (SPMC), 6
Soft goods companies, 46–48, 78
  average life expectancy of, 46
Solomon and Katz, 59–63
Specialization, trend toward (1930s–1940s), 5
Stagemerten, 4
Standard and Poor's Corp., 13
Steelco Company, profit planning program, 164–169
Sterling Insurance Company, 18
STP (oil additive), sales promotion of, 70

Strategic business planning, 181–193
  case histories, 183–192
    market planning, 183–186
    task force assignment, 188–192
  by using individual initiative, 192–193
  economic business cycle, 181–182
Supreme Products, 29–33
Sutton Guild Division, 80–84
Swenson, Eric, 120–121
Swenson Boat Company, profit improvement program, 120–124
  sales volume from, 124
  unclogging communications channels in, 122–123

Taylor, Bud, 88
Taylor, Frederick, 1–2
Taylor Boys (industrial engineers), 3–4
Temporary management systems, 192–193
Thomas, Wes, 71–72
Thomas Register, 13
Titan Carpet Sweeper Company, 20–22
Tracy, Logan, 178–180
Truman, Harry, 152
Truth in Lending Law, 78
Turnaround program, 89–109, 110, 192
  basic approach to, 98
  large corporation, 98–105
  medium-sized company, 89–98
  radical type of, 105–109
  role of management in, 90
  wheeler-dealer type of, 90
Turner, Harry, 65–66
2001: A Space Odyssey, 130

United Mining and Metals, 59
United States Steel Company, 36
Universal Camera Equipment Corporation, 26–27
University of Miami, 42

Vortex Industries, 183–186

Walters, Larry, 49–53
Walton Tobacco Company, turnaround program, 98–105
  overall approach to, 99–101
  programs implemented, 101–105
    control of paper stock, 103–104

Index

Walton Tobacco Company (*Cont.*)
    customer service, 102
    data collection system, 104
    management development, 104–105
    material usage and scrap control,
      104
    materials management, 103
    plant capability study, 101
    production planning and control,
      102–103
    purchasing, 104
    sales reorganization, 101–102
  purpose of, 98
Wandell, Bruce, 187–188
Wankel, Felix, 200
Ward, Les, 38–41

Watson, Tom, 155
Watt, James, 202
Watt, James, Jr., 1
Weldon Chemicals, 162
Westport Manufacturing Company,
    135–138
Whiteside, George, 10–12
Winchester Manufacturing Company,
    86–88
Wolff, Dick, 25–26
Wolfson, Louis, 57
Wood, Franklin, 192–193
Wright, Wilbur and Orville, 198–199,
    202

Xerox Corporation, 151